8.50
Sch

JUL 2000
JUN 2004

WITHDRAWN   JUN 09

JUL X X 2015

WITHDRAWN

The Scarecrow Author Bibliographies

SYLVIA PLATH:
A Bibliography

compiled by

GARY LANE
and
MARIA STEVENS

The Scarecrow Author Bibliographies, No. 36

CUMBERLAND COUNTY COLLEGE
LEARNING RESOURCE CENTER
P. O. BOX 517
VINELAND, N. J. 08360

The Scarecrow Press, Inc.
Metuchen, N.J. & London
1978

Ref
Z
8695.85
L36

78-69

Library of Congress Cataloging in Publication Data

Lane, Gary, 1943-
    Sylvia Plath.

    (The Scarecrow author bibliographies ; no. 36)
    Includes indexes.
    1.   Plath, Sylvia--Bibliography.   I.   Stevens, Maria,
1945-   joint author.
Z8695.85.L36   [PS3566.L27]   016.811'5'4
ISBN 0-8108-1117-0   78-834

Copyright © 1978 by Gary Lane and Maria Stevens

Manufactured in the United States of America

TABLE OF CONTENTS

PREFACE

The work of bibliography--tedious and exacting as it is--has been much lightened for us. A research grant from the University of Texas at San Antonio enabled us to correspond with the editors of periodicals throughout the world and to borrow extensively from American libraries. Earlier bibliographies, including Robin Roberts' unpublished "A Comprehensive Bibliography of Sylvia Plath," gave us a place to start, and the collection of Plath materials at the University of Texas at Austin's Humanities Research Center helped us considerably. Olwyn Hughes, executrix of the Plath Estate, kindly supplied confirmation of several primary items we could not gain access to, and many editors of journals went out of their way not only to confirm items we inquired about but to suggest others. The staffs of the University of Texas System Libraries, both at San Antonio and at Austin, were unfailingly helpful, as was the library staff at Trinity University. And at UTSA we had the expert and cheerfully given assistance of Kathleen Ackermann and Karen Dempsey in preparing the manuscript.

The plan of the work is self-evident and simple, but the fragility of our classification system for secondary materials must be emphasized. It is easy enough to distinguish the seventy-word review of Ariel in, say, Booklist from the scholarly article on Plath's color imagery in PMLA, but the distinction between review and article fades into occasional grayness. Similar but more troublesome vagueness attends the distinction between "popular" and "scholarly" articles, and for this reason we have avoided such classification. No full chronology of the composition dates of Plath's works has yet been established, but we have included, for those interested in her poetic development, a chronology of their publication dates (Appendix A).

It is of course unlikely that we have found and listed every significant appearance of primary materials, and quite certainly we will have missed some secondary ones. "Perfection is terrible," wrote Sylvia Plath, and the bibliographic quest for it, however ardent, is doomed from the start. But we have corrected many errors in previous bibliographies and have confirmed by sight well over 90 per cent of our entries. For a few of the remaining items--all very early ones --we could discover only partial citations; we use them anyway, preferring incompleteness to omission. On these as on all citations here, we will be grateful for additions or corrections.

A year of Fridays, mid-week afternoons, and occasional weekends--of library odysseys, orgies of correspondence, and wakes of proofreading--are enclosed between the covers of this book. We set out to produce, and hope we have succeeded in producing, a useful and reasonably comprehensive reference work. Whatever we have made, the book could not have been done without the kindness and forebearance of Alice Goodwin and Rachel Stevens, of Bonnie Lane, Baron, and Heathcliff.

Gary Lane
Maria Stevens
The University of Texas
at San Antonio
September 1977

I

WORKS BY SYLVIA PLATH

A. BOOKS (CHRONOLOGICAL)
(with contents listed under each)

1   A Winter Ship. Edinburgh: Tragara Press, 1960.
     Limited edition--number of copies printed unknown but
     very small.
        A Winter Ship

2   The Colossus. London: William Heinemann, 1960.
        The Manor Garden
        Two Views of a Cadaver Room
        Night Shift
        Sow
        The Eye-mote
        Hardcastle Crags
        Faun
        Departure
        The Colossus
        Lorelei
        Point Shirley
        The Bull of Bendylaw
        All the Dead Dears
        Aftermath
        The Thin People
        Suicide Off Egg Rock
        Mushrooms
        I Want, I Want
        Watercolour of Grantchester Meadows
        The Ghost's Leavetaking
        Metaphors
        Black Rook in Rainy Weather
        A Winter Ship
        Full Fathom Five
        Maudlin
        Blue Moles
        Strumpet Song

Ouija
Man in Black
Snakecharmer
The Hermit at Outermost House
The Disquieting Muses
Medallion
Two Sisters of Persephone
The Companionable Ills
Moonrise
Spinster
Frog Autumn
Mussel Hunter at Rock Harbour
The Beekeeper's Daughter
The Times Are Tidy
The Burnt-out Spa
Sculptor
Poem for a Birthday
   1. Who
   2. Dark House
   3. Maenad
   4. The Beast
   5. Flute Notes from a Reedy Pond
   6. Witch Burning
   7. The Stones

The Colossus and Other Poems. New York: Alfred A.
Knopf, 1962.   Contents differ from earlier Heinemann
edition.
The Manor Garden
Two Views of a Cadaver Room
Night Shift
Sow
The Eye-mote
Hardcastle Crags
Faun
Departure
The Colossus
Lorelei
Point Shirley
The Bull of Bendylaw
All the Dead Dears
Aftermath
The Thin People
Suicide Off Egg Rock
Mushrooms
I Want, I Want
Watercolor of Grantchester Meadows

The Ghost's Leavetaking
A Winter Ship
Full Fathom Five
Blue Moles
Strumpet Song
Man in Black
Snakecharmer
The Hermit at Outermost House
The Disquieting Muses
Medallion
The Companionable Ills
Moonrise
Spinster
Frog Autumn
Mussel Hunter at Rock Harbor
The Beekeeper's Daughter
The Times Are Tidy
The Burnt-out Spa
Sculptor
Flute Notes from a Reedy Pond
The Stones

4   The Colossus. London: Faber & Faber, 1967. Contents identical to earlier Heinemann edition.

5   The Colossus and Other Poems. New York: Random
House, 1968 (paperback). Contents identical to earlier
Knopf edition.

6   The Colossus. London: Faber & Faber, 1972 (paper
back). Contents identical to earlier British editions.

7   The Bell Jar. London: William Heinemann, 1963.
This edition published under the pseudonym, Victoria
Lucas.

8   The Bell Jar. London: Faber & Faber, 1966.

9   The Bell Jar. London: Faber & Faber, 1966 (paper
back).

10   The Bell Jar. New York: Harper & Row, 1971. With
a biographical note by Lois Ames and eight drawings by
Sylvia Plath.

11   The Bell Jar. New York: Bantam, 1972 (paperback).
With a biographical note by Lois Ames and eight drawings by Sylvia Plath.

12   Uncollected Poems. London: Turret Books, 1965.
     Limited edition of 150 copies. With a jacket drawing
     by Sylvia Plath.
              Blackberrying
              Wuthering Heights
              A Life
              Crossing the Wate
              Private Ground
              An Appearance
              Half Moon (holograph)
              Finisterre
              Insomniac
              I Am Vertical
              Candles
              Parliament Hill Fields

13   Ariel. London: Faber & Faber, 1965.
              Morning Song
              The Couriers
              Sheep in Fog
              The Applicant
              Lady Lazarus
              Tulips
              Cut
              Elm
              The Night Dances
              Poppies in October
              Berck-Plage
              Ariel
              Death & Co.
              Nick and the Candlestick
              Gulliver
              Getting There
              Medusa
              The Moon and the Yew Tree
              A Birthday Present
              Letter in November
              The Rival
              Daddy
              You're
              Fever 103°
              The Bee Meeting
              The Arrival of the Bee Box
              Stings
              Wintering
              The Hanging Man
              Little Fugue

Years
The Munich Mannequins
Totem
Paralytic
Balloons
Poppies in July
Kindness
Contusion
Edge
Words

14   Ariel. New York: Harper & Row, 1966. With a fore-
word by Robert Lowell. Contents differ from earlier
Faber & Faber edition.
Morning Song
The Couriers
Sheep in Fog
The Applicant
Lady Lazarus
Tulips
Cut
Elm
The Night Dances
Poppies in October
Berck-Plage
Ariel
Death & Co.
Lesbos
Nick and the Candlestick
Gulliver
Getting There
Medusa
The Moon and the Yew Tree
A Birthday Present
Mary's Song
Letter in November
The Rival
Daddy
You're
Fever 103°
The Bee Meeting
The Arrival of the Bee Box
Stings
The Swarm
Wintering
The Hanging Man
Little Fugue

Years
The Munich Mannequins
Totem
Paralytic
Balloons
Poppies in July
Kindness
Contusion
Edge
Words

15 Ariel. New York: Harper & Row, 1966 (paperback).
Contents identical to earlier Harper & Row edition.

16 Ariel. London: Faber & Faber, 1968 (paperback).
Contents identical to earlier Faber & Faber edition.

17 Three Women: A Monologue for Three Voices. London:
Turret Books, 1968. Limited edition of 180 copies.
With a preface by Douglas Cleverdon.
Three Women

18 Wreath for a Bridal. Frensham, England: Sceptre
Press, 1970. Limited edition of 100 copies.
Wreath for a Bridal

19 Million Dollar Month. Frensham, England: Sceptre
Press, 1971. Limited edition of 150 copies.
Million Dollar Month

20 Child. Exeter, England: Rougemont Press, 1971. Limited edition of 325 copies.
Child

21 Fiesta Melons. Exeter, England: Rougemont Press,
1971. Limited edition of 150 copies. With an introduc-
tion by Ted Hughes and 11 drawings by Sylvia Plath.
Green Rock, Winthrop Bay
Two Lovers and a Beachcomber by the Real Sea
Battle-Scene from the Comic Operatic Fantasy 'The
Seafarer'
Complaint of the Crazed Queen
Dream of the Hearse-Driver
Southern Sunrise
Fiesta Melons
The Surgeon at 2 a.m.
November Graveyard

Yadwigha, on a Red Couch, Among Lilies (A Sestina
for the Douanier)

22 Crystal Gazer. London: Rainbow Press, 1971. Lim-
ited edition of 400 copies. With a frontispiece drawing
by Sylvia Plath.
Ballade Banale
Alicante Lullaby
Leaving Early
Notes on Zarathustra's Prologue
Mad Girl's Love Song
On the Plethora of Dryads
The Dream of the Hearse-Driver
Go Get the Goodly Squab
The Beggars
Circus in Three Rings
The Goring
Admonition
Recantation
Crystal Gazer
Stopped Dead
Mirror
Face Lift
Zoo Keeper's Wife
Heavy Women
Last Words
Fable of the Rhododendron Stealers
Lament
Yadwigha, on a Red Couch, Among Lilies (A Sestina
for the Douanier)

23 Lyonnesse. London: Rainbow Press, 1971. Limited
edition of 400 copies.
A Winter's Tale
Mayflower
Epitaph for Fire and Flower
Old Ladies' Home
Wreath for a Bridal
Metamorphoses of the Moon
Owl
Child
Electra on the Azalea Path
In Midas' Country
Tinker Jack and the Tidy Wives
Two Campers in Cloud Country
The Rabbit Catcher
The Detective

On the Difficulty of Conjuring up a Dryad
The Snowman on the Moor
Widow
The Other Two
Gigolo
Brasilia
Lyonnesse

24 Crossing the Water. London: Faber & Faber, 1971.
    Wuthering Heights
    Pheasant
    Crossing the Water
    Finisterre
    Face Lift
    Parliament Hill Fields
    Insomniac
    An Appearance
    Blackberrying
    I Am Vertical
    The Babysitters
    In Plaster
    Leaving Early
    Stillborn
    Private Ground
    Heavy Women
    Widow
    Magi
    Candles
    Event
    Love Letter
    Small Hours
    Sleep in the Mojave Desert
    The Surgeon at 2 a. m.
    Two Campers in Cloud Country
    Mirror
    A Life
    On Deck
    Apprehensions
    Zoo Keeper's Wife
    Whitsun
    The Tour
    Last Words
    Among the Narcissi

25 Crossing the Water. New York: Harper & Row, 1971.
    Contents differ from Faber & Faber edition.
    Wuthering Heights

Finisterre
Face Lift
Parliament Hill Fields
Heavy Women
Insomniac
I Am Vertical
Blackberrying
The Babysitters
In Plaster
Leaving Early
Stillborn
Private Ground
Widow
Candles
Magi
Love Letter
Small Hours
Sleep in the Mojave Desert
The Surgeon at 2 a.m.
Two Campers in Cloud Country
Mirror
On Deck
Whitsun
Zoo Keeper's Wife
Last Words
Black Rook in Rainy Weather
Metaphors
Maudlin
Ouija
Two Sisters of Persephone
Who
Dark House
Maenad
The Beast
Witch Burning
A Life
Crossing the Water

26 Crossing the Water. New York: Harper & Row, 1975
(paperback).   Contents identical to earlier Harper & Row
edition.

27 Crossing the Water. London: Faber & Faber, 1975 (paperback).   Contents identical to earlier Faber & Faber
edition.

28 Winter Trees. London: Faber & Faber, 1971.
        Winter Trees
        Child
        Brasilia
        Gigolo
        Childless Woman
        Purdah
        The Courage of Shutting-Up
        The Other
        Stopped Dead
        The Rabbit Catcher
        Mystic
        By Candlelight
        Lyonnesse
        Thalidomide
        For a Fatherless Son
        Lesbos
        The Swarm
        Mary's Song
        Three Women

29 Winter Trees. New York: Harper & Row, 1972. Con-
    tents differ from earlier Faber & Faber edition.
        Apprehensions
        Mystic
        Gigolo
        The Courage of Shutting-Up
        An Appearance
        Brasilia
        The Detective
        Among the Narcissi
        Event
        Stopped Dead
        Child
        Amnesiac
        The Other
        Thalidomide
        Eavesdropper
        Pheasant
        By Candlelight
        Lyonnesse
        For a Fatherless Son
        Childless Woman
        The Rabbit Catcher
        The Tour
        Purdah
        Winter Trees
        Three Women

30 Winter Trees. London: Faber & Faber, 1975 (paper-
    back). Contents identical to earlier Faber & Faber edi-
    tion.

31 Pursuit. London: Rainbow Press, 1973. Limited edi-
    tion of 150 copies. With an introduction by Ted Hughes
    and etchings by Leonard Baskin.
        Dark Wood, Dark Water
        Resolve
        Temper of Time
        The Shrike
        Faun
        The Lady and the Earthenware Head
        Pursuit
        Doomsday
        Words Heard, by Accident, over the Phone
        Stings (2)
        Spider
        The Fearful
        The Rival (2)
        A Secret
        Burning the Letters

32 Letters Home: Correspondence 1950-1963, edited and
    with commentary by Aurelia Schober Plath. New York:
    Harper & Row, 1975.

33 Letters Home: Correspondence 1950-1963, edited and
    with commentary by Aurelia Schober Plath. New York:
    Bantam, 1977 (paperback).

34 The Bed Book. London: Faber & Faber, 1976. Illus-
    trations by Quentin Blake. (For children.)

35 The Bed Book. New York: Harper & Row, 1976. Il-
    lustrations by Emily Arnold McCully. (For children.)

36 Johnny Panic and the Bible of Dreams, and Other Prose
    Writings. London: Faber & Faber, 1977. With an in-
    troduction by Ted Hughes.
        Johnny Panic and the Bible of Dreams
        America! America!
        The Day Mr. Prescott Died
        The Wishing Box
        A Comparison
        The Fifteen-Dollar Eagle
        The Daughters of Blossom Street

B. PUBLISHED POEMS

Reference is made to periodicals, Plath's books,
The Art of Sylvia Plath ed. Charles Newman
(Bloomington: Indiana University Press, 1970;
London: Faber & Faber, 1970), and selected an-
thologies (which are designated by the omission of
an underscore). Publication data for the antholo-
gies are available in Appendix D.

37 "Above the Oxbow"
Christian Science Monitor, 4 May 1959, 8

38 "Admonition" (also see "Warning")
Smith Review, Spring 1954, 3
Harvard Advocate, 101 (May 1967), 2
Crystal Gazer (1971)

39 "Aerialist"
Cambridge Review, 90 (7 February 1969), 245

40 "Aftermath"
Arts in Society, 1 (Fall 1959), 66
The Colossus (1960)

41 "Alicante Lullaby"
Crystal Gazer (1971)

42 "All the Dead Dears"
Grécourt Review, 1 (November 1957), 36-37
The Colossus (1960)

43 "Amnesiac"
The New Yorker, 39 (3 August 1963), 29
Winter Trees (American edition only, 1972)
The New Yorker Book of Poems (1974)

44 "Among the Narcissi"
    The New Yorker, 39 (3 August 1963), 29
    Crossing the Water (British edition only, 1971)
    Winter Trees (American edition only, 1972)

45 "Apotheosis"
    The Lyric, 36 (Winter 1956), 10

46 "An Appearance"
    Uncollected Poems (1965)
    Times Literary Supplement, 20 January 1966, 42
    The Art of Sylvia Plath (1970), 254
    Crossing the Water (British edition only, 1971)
    Winter Trees (American edition only, 1972)

47 "The Applicant"
    London Magazine, New Series 2 (January 1963), 15-16.
    Ariel (1965)
    The Honey and the Gall (1967)
    The New Poetry (1967)
    Naked Poetry (1969)
    The Modern Poets (1970)
    Possibilities of Poetry (1970)
    Psyche (1973)
    50 Modern American and British Poets (1973)

48 "Apprehensions"
    The New Yorker, 47 (6 March 1971), 37
    Crossing the Water (British edition only, 1971)
    Winter Trees (American edition only, 1972)

49 "Ariel" (also see "The Horse")
    The Review, 9 (October 1963), 12
    Ariel (1965)
    100 Postwar Poems (1968)
    The College Anthology of British and American
        Poetry (1972)
    The Experience of Poems (1972)
    The Norton Anthology of Modern Poetry (1973)
    Psyche (1973)
    The Norton Anthology of Poetry (Revised, 1975)
    Modern Poems (1976)

50 "The Arrival of the Bee Box"
    Atlantic, 211 (April 1963), 70
    Ariel (1965)
    Poems of Our Moment (1968)

Naked Poetry (1969)
To Play Man Number One (1969)

51 "The Babysitters"
    The New Yorker, 47 (6 March 1971), 36
    Crossing the Water (1971)

52 "Ballade Banale"
    Crystal Gazer (1971)

53 "Balloons"
    Ariel (1965)
    To Play Man Number One (1969)

54 "Bathtub Battle Scene" (also see "Battle-Scene from the
    Comic Operatic Fantasy 'The Seafarer'")
    Christian Science Monitor, 25 April 1959, 12

55 "Battle-Scene from the Comic Operatic Fantasy 'The Sea-
    farer'" (also see "Bathtub Battle Scene")
    Times Literary Supplement, 31 July 1969, 855
    The Art of Sylvia Plath (1970), 246-247
    Fiesta Melons (1971)

56 "The Beast" (part IV of "Poem for a Birthday")
    The Colossus (British editions only, 1960)
    Crossing the Water (American editions only, 1971)

57 "The Bee Meeting"
    London Magazine, New Series 3 (April 1963), 24-25
    Critical Quarterly Supplement Number Six (1965), 2-3
    Ariel (1965)
    Tri-Quarterly, 7 (Fall 1966), 29-31
    Poems of Our Moment (1968)

58 "The Beekeeper's Daughter"
    Kenyon Review, 22 (Autumn 1960), 595
    The Colossus (1960)

59 "The Beggars"
    Chelsea, 7 (May 1960), 70
    Critical Quarterly, 2 (Summer 1960), 156
    Crystal Gazer (1971)

60 "Berck-Plage"
    London Magazine, New Series 3 (June 1963), 26-31
    Ariel (1965)

61 "A Birthday Present"
   Critical Quarterly, 5 (Spring 1963), 3-4
   Ariel (1965)

62 "Bitter Strawberries"
   Christian Science Monitor, 11 August 1950, 17

63 "Black Rook in Rainy Weather"
   Granta, 61 (18 May 1957), 9
   Antioch Review, 17 (June 1957), 232-233
   London Magazine, 5 (June 1958), 47-48
   The Colossus (British editions only, 1960)
   New Poets of England and America (1962)
   Poems of Doubt and Belief (1964)
   Poems on Poetry (1965)
   A Little Treasury of Modern Poetry (1970)
   Mademoiselle, 73 (September 1971), 161
   Crossing the Water (American editions only, 1971)
   Psyche (1973)
   The Norton Anthology of Poetry (Revised, 1975)

64 "Blackberrying"
   The New Yorker, 38 (15 September 1962), 48
   Uncollected Poems (1965)
   Crossing the Water (1971)
   The Norton Anthology of Modern Poetry (1973)
   The New Yorker Book of Poems (1974)

65 "Blue Moles"
   Critical Quarterly, 2 (Summer 1960), 156-157
   The Colossus (1960)
   New Poets of England and America (1962)
   The Poem (1968)

66 "Brasilia"
   The Review, 9 (October 1963), 15
   Lyonnesse (1971)
   Winter Trees (1971)
   Contemporary American Poetry (1975)

67 "The Bull of Bendylaw"
   Horn Book, 35 (April 1959), 148
   The Colossus (1960)

68 "Burning the Letters"
   Pursuit (1973)

69   "The Burnt-out Spa"
         The Colossus (1960)

70   "By Candlelight"
         The New Yorker, 47 (6 March 1971), 37
         London Magazine, New Series 11 (September 1971),
            44-45
         Winter Trees (1971)

71   "Candles"
         The Listener, 64 (17 November 1960), 877
         Uncollected Poems (1965)
         Crossing the Water (1971)

72   "Child"
         The New Statesman, 65 (3 May 1963), 683
         A Flock of Words (1969)
         Child (1971)
         Lyonnesse (1971)
         Winter Trees (1971)

73   "Childless Woman"
         Encounter, 21 (October 1963), 50
         Winter Trees (1971)

74   "Circus in Three Rings"
         Smith Review, Fall 1954, 18
         Atlantic, 196 (August 1955), 68
         Harvard Advocate, 101 (May 1967), 3
         Crystal Gazer (1971)

75   "The Colossus"
         Kenyon Review, 22 (Autumn 1960), 596
         The Colossus (1960)
         New Poets of England and America (1962)
         Encounter, 18 (April 1962), 56
         Tri-Quarterly, 7 (Fall 1966), 14-15
         A Little Treasury of Modern Poetry (1970)
         Possibilities of Poetry (1970)
         Psyche (1973)
         The Norton Anthology of Modern Poetry (1973)
         Contemporary American Poetry (1975)

76   "The Companionable Ills"
         The Spectator, 202 (30 January 1959), 163
         The Colossus (1960)

77   "Complaint of the Crazed Queen"
      Times Literary Supplement, 31 July 1969, 855

78   "Contusion"
      The Observer, 17 February 1963, 23
      Ariel (1965)

79   "The Courage of Shutting-Up"
      The New Yorker, 47 (6 March 1971), 36-37.
      London Magazine, New Series 11 (September 1971), 41+.
      Winter Trees (1971)

80   "The Couriers"
      London Magazine, New Series 3 (April 1963), 30-31
      Ariel (1965)

81   "Crossing the Water"
      The Observer, 23 September 1962, 25
      Uncollected Poems (1965)
      Intellectual Digest, 2 (November 1971), 95
      Crossing the Water (1971)

82   "Crystal Gazer"
      Crystal Gazer (1971)

83   "Cut"
      London Magazine, New Series 3 (April 1963), 28-29
      Ariel (1965)
      Tri-Quarterly, 7 (Fall 1966), 28-29
      The College Anthology of British and American Poet-
          ry (1972)
      Contemporary American Poetry (1975)

84   "Daddy"
      Encounter, 21 (October 1963), 52
      The Review, 9 (October 1963), 4-6
      Critical Quarterly Supplement Number Five (1964),
          2-4
      Ariel (1965)
      Time, 87 (10 June 1966), 118
      Tri-Quarterly, 7 (Fall 1966), 32-34
      The New Poetry (1967)
      100 Postwar Poems (1968)
      Naked Poetry (1969)
      The Contemporary American Poets (1969)
      Possibilities of Poetry (1970)
      The Modern Poets (1970)
      A Little Treasury of Modern Poetry (1970)

Psyche (1973)
The Norton Anthology of Modern Poetry (1973)
50 Modern American and British Poets (1973)
Contemporary American Poetry (1975)
Modern Poems (1976)

85 "Danse Macabre"
    Smith Review, Spring 1955, 12
    Harvard Advocate, 101 (May 1967), 2

86 "Dark House" (part II of "Poem for a Birthday")
    The Colossus (British editions only, 1960).
    Crossing the Water (American editions only, 1971)

87 "Dark Wood, Dark Water"
    Christian Science Monitor, 17 December 1959, 12
    Pursuit (1973)

88 "Death & Co."
    Encounter, 21 (October 1963), 45
    Ariel (1965)
    Tri-Quarterly, 7 (Fall 1966), 31-32
    100 Postwar Poems (1968)
    Poems of Our Moment (1968)

89 "The Death of Mythmaking"
    Poetry, 94 (September 1959), 370
    Tri-Quarterly, 7 (Fall 1966), 11

90 "Denouement"
    Smith Review, Spring 1954, 23

91 "Departure"
    The Nation, 188 (7 March 1959), 212
    The Colossus (1960)

92 "Departure of the Ghost" (also see "The Ghost's Leave-
    taking")
    Sewanee Review, 67 (July-September 1959), 446-447

93 "The Detective"
    Lyonnesse (1971)
    Winter Trees (American edition only, 1972)

94 "Dialogue en Route"
    Smith Review, Spring 1955, 12-13
    Harvard Advocate, 101 (May 1967), 3

By Sylvia Plath   20

Times Literary Supplement, 31 July 1969, 855
The Art of Sylvia Plath (1970), 239-240

95 "The Disquieting Muses"
    London Magazine, 6 (March 1959), 35-36
    The Colossus (1960)

96 "Doomsday"
    Smith Review, Spring 1953, 22
    Harper's, 208 (May 1954), 29
    Harvard Advocate, 101 (May 1967), 2
    Pursuit (1973)

97 "Dream of the Hearse-Driver"
    Times Literary Supplement, 31 July 1969, 855
    Fiesta Melons (1971)
    Crystal Gazer (1971)

98 "Dream with Clam Diggers"
    Poetry, 89 (January 1957), 232-233
    Granta, 61 (9 March 1957), 5

99 "Eavesdropper"
    Poetry, 102 (August 1963), 296-298
    Winter Trees (American edition only, 1972)

100 "Edge"
     The Observer, 17 February 1963, 23
     Ariel (1965)
     Intellectual Digest, 2 (November 1971), 95

101 "Electra on the Azalea Path"
     Hudson Review, 13 (Autumn 1960), 414-415
     Lyonnesse (1971)

102 "Ella Mason and Her Eleven Cats"
     Granta, 60 (10 November 1956), 25
     Poetry, 90 (July 1957), 233-234

103 "Elm" (also see "The Elm Speaks")
     Ariel (1965)
     The Poem (1968)
     Possibilities of Poetry (1970)
     The Norton Anthology of Modern Poetry (1973)

104 "The Elm Speaks (also see "Elm")
     The New Yorker, 39 (3 August 1963), 28
     The New Yorker Book of Poems (1974)

105 "Epitaph for Fire and Flower"
     Poetry, 89 (January 1957), 236-237
     The Art of Sylvia Plath (1970), 244-245
     Lyonnesse (1971)

106 "Event"
     The Observer, 16 December 1962, 21
     Crossing the Water (British edition only, 1971)
     Winter Trees (American edition only, 1972)

107 "The Eye-mote"
     Chelsea, 7 (May 1960), 71
     The Colossus (1960)

108 "Fable of the Rhododendron Stealers"
     Crystal Gazer (1971)

109 "Face Lift"
     Poetry, 99 (March 1962), 349
     Crystal Gazer (1971)
     Crossing the Water (1971)

110 "Faun" (also see "Metamorphosis")
     The Colossus (1960)
     Pursuit (1973)

111 "The Fearful"
     The Observer, 17 February 1963, 23
     Pursuit (1973)

112 "Fever 103°"
     Poetry, 102 (August 1963), 292-294
     The Review, 9 (October 1963), 10-11
     Ariel (1965)
     Tri-Quarterly, 7 (Fall 1966), 26-27
     The New Poetry (1967)
     The Norton Anthology of Modern Poetry (1973)

113 "Fiesta Melons"
     Fiesta Melons (1971)

114 "Finisterre"
     The Observer, 5 August 1962, 14
     Uncollected Poems (1965)
     Crossing the Water (1971)

115 "Flute Notes from a Reedy Pond" (part V of "Poem for
     a Birthday")
     Texas Quarterly, 3 (Winter 1960), 120

The Colossus (1960)

116 "For a Fatherless Son"
     Critical Quarterly, 5 (Summer 1963), 115
     The New Yorker, 47 (6 March 1971), 37
     London Magazine, New Series 11 (September 1971),
     42-43
     Winter Trees (1971)

117 "Frog Autumn"
     The Nation, 188 (24 January 1959), 74
     The Colossus (1960)

118 "Full Fathom Five"
     Audience, 6 (Spring 1959), 34-35
     London Magazine, 7 (June 1960), 12-13
     The Colossus (1960)

119 "Getting There"
     Encounter, 21 (October 1963), 47-48
     Ariel (1965)

120 "The Ghost's Leavetaking" (also see "Departure of the
     Ghost")
     The Colossus (1960)
     New Poets of England and America (1962)

121 "Gigolo"
     The New Yorker, 46 (21 November 1970), 54
     London Magazine, New Series 11 (September 1971),
     45-46
     Lyonnesse (1971)
     Winter Trees (1971)

122 "Go Get the Goodly Squab"
     Harper's, 209 (November 1954), 47
     Crystal Gazer (1971)

123 "The Goring"
     Arts in Society, 1 (Fall 1959), 66
     Crystal Gazer (1971)

124 "Green Rock, Winthrop Bay"
     Fiesta Melons (1971)

125 "Gulliver"
     Ariel (1965)

126 "Half Moon" (early version of what became "Thalido-
     mide")
          Uncollected Poems (1965)
          The Art of Sylvia Plath (1970), 273-279

127 "The Hanging Man"
          Ariel (1965)
          A College Book of Verse (1970)

128 "Hardcastle Crags" (also see "Night Walk")
          The Colossus (1960)
          The Golden Year (1960)

129 "Heavy Women"
          Poetry, 99 (March 1962), 350
          Crystal Gazer (1971)
          Crossing the Water (1971)

130 "The Hermit at Outermost House"
          Audience, 6 (Spring 1959), 36
          Times Literary Supplement, 6 November 1959,
               xxix
          The Colossus (1960)

131 "The Horse" (also see "Ariel")
          The Observer, 3 November 1963, 22

132 "I Am Vertical"
          Critical Quarterly, 3 (Summer 1961), 140-141
          Uncollected Poems (1965)
          Crossing the Water (1971)

133 "I Want, I Want"
          Partisan Review, 26 (Fall 1959), 558
          The Colossus (1960)

134 "In Midas' Country"
          London Magazine, 6 (October 1959), 11
          Lyonnesse (1971)

135 "In Plaster"
          London Magazine, New Series 1 (February 1962),
               15-17
          Critical Quarterly Supplement Number Five (1964),
               3-4
          Tri-Quarterly, 7 (Fall 1966), 16-18
          The Art of Sylvia Plath (1970), 252-253
          Crossing the Water (1971)

136 "Insomniac"
     Uncollected Poems (1965)
     Crossing the Water (1971)

137 "The Jailor"
     Encounter, 21 (October 1963), 51
     Male and Female (1972)

138 "Kindness"
     The Observer, 17 February 1963, 23
     Ariel (1965)
     Psyche (1973)
     A Book of Comfort (1974)

139 "The Lady and the Earthenware Head"
     Pursuit (1973)

140 "Lady Lazarus"
     Encounter, 21 (October 1963), 49
     The Review, 9 (October 1965), 7-9
     Critical Quarterly Supplement Number Six (1965),
         3-5
     Ariel (1965)
     Tri-Quarterly, 7 (Fall 1966), 35-37
     Naked Poetry (1969)
     Possibilities of Poetry (1970)
     Intellectual Digest, 2 (November 1971), 95
     Psyche (1973)
     The Norton Anthology of Modern Poetry (1973)
     The Norton Anthology of Poetry (Revised, 1975)
     Contemporary American Poetry (1975)
     Modern Poems (1976)

141 "Lament"
     New Orleans Poetry Journal, 1 (October 1955), 19
     Crystal Gazer (1971)

142 "Last Words"
     Crystal Gazer (1971)
     Crossing the Water (1971)

143 "Leaving Early"
     London Magazine, New Series 1 (August 1961), 9-10
     Harper's, 225 (December 1962), 82
     Crystal Gazer (1971)
     Crossing the Water (1971)

144 "Lesbos"
     The Review, 9 (October 1963), 17-19
     New York Review of Books, 6 (12 May 1966), 4-5
     Tri-Quarterly, 7 (Fall 1966), 18-20
     Ariel (American editions only, 1966)
     The Art of Sylvia Plath (1970), 255-257
     Winter Trees (British edition only, 1971)

145 "A Lesson in Vengeance"
     Poetry, 94 (September 1959), 371

146 "Letter in November"
     London Magazine, New Series 3 (April 1963), 29-30
     Ariel (1965)

147 "Letter to a Purist"
     Times Literary Supplement, 31 July 1969, 855

148 "A Life"
     The Listener, 65 (4 May 1961), 776
     Uncollected Poems (1965)
     Crossing the Water (1971)

149 "Little Fugue"
     Encounter, 21 (October 1963), 50
     Ariel (1965)

150 "Lorelei"
     London Magazine, 6 (March 1959), 34-35
     Audience, 6 (Spring 1959), 33
     The Colossus (1960)

151 "Love Letter"
     Poetry, 99 (March 1962), 350-351
     Crossing the Water (1971)

152 "Lyonnesse"
     The Observer, 10 May 1970, 31
     Lyonnesse (1971)
     Winter Trees (1971)

153 "Mad Girl's Love Song"
     Smith Review, Spring 1953, 13
     Mademoiselle, 37 (August 1953), 358
     Granta, 61 (4 May 1957), 19
     Harvard Advocate, 101 (May 1967), 3
     Crystal Gazer (1971)

154 "Maenad" (part III of "Poem for a Birthday")
     The Colossus (British editions only, 1960)
     Crossing the Water (American editions only, 1971)

155 "Magi"
     The New Statesman, 61 (31 March 1961), 514
     Crossing the Water (1971)

156 "Main Street at Midnight" (also see "Owl")
     The Spectator, 202 (13 February 1959), 227

157 "Man in Black"
     The New Yorker, 36 (9 April 1960), 40
     The Colossus (1960)

158 "The Manor Garden"
     Critical Quarterly, 2 (Summer 1960), 155
     Atlantic, 206 (September 1960), 52
     The Colossus (1960)

159 "Mary's Song"
     London Magazine, New Series 3 (April 1963), 31
     The Review, 9 (October 1963), 16
     Ariel (American editions only, 1966)
     Winter Trees (British edition only, 1971)
     Contemporary American Poetry (1975)

160 "Maudlin"
     The Colossus (British editions only, 1960)
     Crossing the Water (American editions only, 1971)

161 "Mayflower"
     Lyonnesse (1971)

162 "Medallion"
     Critical Quarterly Supplement Number One (1960),
     20
     The Colossus (1960)
     The Norton Anthology of Poetry (1970)

163 "Medusa"
     Ariel (1965)
     Contemporary American Poetry (1975)

164 "Memoirs of a Spinach Picker"
     Christian Science Monitor, 29 December 1959, 8

165   "Metamorphoses of the Moon"
        Lyonnesse (1971)

166   "Metamorphosis" (also see "Faun")
        Poetry, 89 (January 1957), 234
        Poetry, 121 (October 1972), 25

167   "Metaphors" (also see "Metaphors for a Pregnant Wo-
        man")
        The Colossus (British editions only, 1960)
        Crossing the Water (American editions only, 1971)

168   "Metaphors for a Pregnant Woman" (also see "Meta-
        phors")
        Partisan Review, 27 (Summer 1960), 435

169   "Million Dollar Month"
        Million Dollar Month (1971)

170   "Mirror"
        The New Yorker, 39 (3 August 1963), 29
        Crystal Gazer (1971)
        Crossing the Water (1971)
        The New Yorker Book of Poems (1974)

171   "Miss Drake Proceeds to Supper"
        Chequer, No. 11 (Winter 1956/57), 0
        The Art of Sylvia Plath (1970), 241

172   "Mojave Desert" (also see "Sleep in the Mojave Desert")
        The Observer, 19 November 1961, 28

173   "The Moon and the Yew Tree"
        The New Yorker, 39 (3 August 1963), 29
        Ariel (1965)
        The Contemporary American Poets (1969)
        Naked Poetry (1969)
        The New Yorker Book of Poems (1974)

174   "Moonrise"
        Hudson Review, 13 (Autumn 1960), 416
        The Colossus (1960)

175   "Morning Song"
        Ariel (1965)
        A College Book of Verse (1970)
        Redbook, 140 (January 1973), 76
        50 Modern American and British Poets (1973)

176   "The Munich Mannequins"
      New York Review of Books, 2 (20 February 1964), 13
      Ariel (1965)
      Naked Poetry (1969)

177   "Mushrooms"
      Harper's, 221 (July 1960), 25
      New Poets of England and America (1962)
      The Colossus (1965)
      Tri-Quarterly, 7 (Fall 1966), 15
      A Book of Nature Poems (1969)
      The Art of Sylvia Plath (1970), 250-251
      Psyche (1973)

178   "Mussel Hunter at Rock Harbor"
      The New Yorker, 34 (9 August 1958), 22
      The Colossus (1960)
      The New Yorker Book of Poems (1974)

179   "Mystic"
      The New Yorker, 39 (3 August 1963), 28-29
      The Art of Sylvia Plath (1970), 260
      Winter Trees (1971)
      The New Yorker Book of Poems (1974)

180   "Natural History"
      Cambridge Review, 90 (7 February 1969), 244-245

181   "The Net Menders"
      The New Yorker, 36 (20 August 1960), 36

182   "Nick and the Candlestick"
      The Review, 9 (October 1963), 13-14
      Ariel (1965)
      Tri-Quarterly, 7 (Fall 1966), 22-23
      The Contemporary American Poets (1969)
      Contemporary American Poetry (1975)

183   "The Night Dances"
      Ariel (1965)
      Poems of Our Moment (1968)

184   "Night Shift"
      The Colossus (1960)

185   "Night Walk" (also see "Hardcastle Crags")
      The New Yorker, 34 (11 October 1958), 40

The New Yorker Book of Poems (1974)

186 "Notes on Zarathustra's Prologue"
     Crystal Gazer (1971)

187 "November Graveyard"
     Mademoiselle, 62 (November 1965), 134
     Fiesta Melons (1971)

188 "Ode to a Bitten Plum"
     Seventeen, 33 (January 1974), 136

189 "Old Ladies' Home"
     Lyonnesse (1971)

190 "On Deck"
     The New Yorker, 37 (22 July 1961), 32
     Critical Quarterly, 12 (Summer 1970), 150
     Crossing the Water (1971)

191 "On the Decline of Oracles"
     Poetry, 94 (September 1959), 368-369

192 "On the Difficulty of Conjuring Up a Dryad"
     Chequer, No. 11 (Winter 1956/57), 4
     Poetry, 90 (July 1957), 235-236
     Lyonnesse (1971)

193 "On the Plethora of Dryads"
     New Mexico Quarterly, 27 (Spring-Summer 1957),
       211-212
     The Art of Sylvia Plath (1970), 242-243
     Crystal Gazer (1971)

194 "The Other"
     Encounter, 21 (October 1963), 47
     Winter Trees (1971)

195 "The Other Two"
     Lyonnesse (1971)

196 "Ouija"
     Hudson Review, 13 (Autumn 1960), 413
     The Colossus (British editions only, 1960)
     Crossing the Water (American editions only, 1971)

197 "Owl" (also see "Main Street at Midnight")
     Lyonnesse (1971)

198 "Paralytic"
     Ariel (1965)

199 "Parliament Hill Fields"
     London Magazine, New Series 1 (August 1961), 7-8
     Critical Quarterly Supplement Number Three (1962),
        10
     Uncollected Poems (1965)
     Crossing the Water (1971)

200 "Pheasant"
     The New Yorker, 47 (6 March 1971), 36
     Crossing the Water (British edition only, 1971)
     Winter Trees (American edition only, 1972)

201 "Poem for a Birthday" (also see titles of individual sec-
     tions of the poem: "The Beast," "Dark House," "Flute
     Notes from a Reedy Pond," "Maenad," "The Stones,"
     "Who," and "Witch Burning")
     The Colossus (British editions only, 1960)

202 "Point Shirley"
     Sewanee Review, 67 (July-September 1959), 447-448
     The Colossus (1960)
     The Norton Anthology of Poetry (1970)

203 "Poppies in July"
     Ariel (1965)
     Naked Poetry (1969)

204 "Poppies in October"
     The Observer, 6 October 1963, 24
     The Review, 9 (October 1963), 13
     Ariel (1965)
     The Norton Anthology of Modern Poetry (1973)

205 "Private Ground"
     Critical Quarterly, 3 (Summer 1961), 140
     Harper's, 225 (August 1962), 55
     Uncollected Poems (1965)
     Crossing the Water (1971)

206 "Prologue to Spring"
     Christian Science Monitor, 23 March 1959, 8

207 "Purdah"
     Poetry, 102 (August 1963), 294-296
     The Art of Sylvia Plath (1970), 258-259
     Winter Trees (1971)

208 "Pursuit"
     Atlantic, 199 (January 1957), 65
     Pursuit (1973)

209 "The Rabbit Catcher"
     Lyonnesse (1971)
     Winter Trees (1971)

210 "Recantation"
     Accent, 17 (Autumn 1957), 247
     Crystal Gazer (1971)

211 "Resolve"
     Granta, 61 (9 March 1957), 5
     Cambridge Review, 90 (7 February 1969), 244-245
     Pursuit (1973)

212 "The Rival" [1]
     The Observer, 21 January 1962, 31
     Ariel (1965)
     The Norton Anthology of Poetry (1970)

213 "The Rival" [2]
     Pursuit (1973)

214 "Sculptor"
     Grécourt Review, 2 (May 1959), 282
     Arts in Society, 1 (Fall 1959), 67
     The Colossus (1960)
     Tri-Quarterly, 7 (Fall 1966), 16

215 "Second Winter"
     The Lyric, 36 (Winter 1956), 11
     Ladies' Home Journal, 75 (December 1958), 143

216 "A Secret"
     Pursuit (1973)

217 "Sheep in Fog"
     Ariel (1965)
     Naked Poetry (1969)

218 "The Shrike"
     Pursuit (1973)

219 "Sleep in the Mojave Desert" (also see "Mojave Desert")
     Harper's, 224 (February 1962), 36
     Crossing the Water (1971)

220 "The Sleepers"
     London Magazine, 7 (June 1960), 11

221 "Small Hours"
     London Magazine, New Series 1 (August 1961), 7
     Critical Quarterly Supplement Number Five (1964),
         2
     Crossing the Water (1971)

222 "Snakecharmer"
     London Magazine, 6 (March 1959), 33-34
     The Colossus (1960)
     New Poets of England and America (1962)
     Poems on Poetry (1965)

223 "The Snowman on the Moor"
     Poetry, 90 (July 1957), 229-231
     Lyonnesse (1971)

224 "Soliloquy of the Solipsist"
     Granta, 61 (4 May 1957), 19

225 "Song for a Summer Day"
     Christian Science Monitor, 18 August 1959, 8

226 "Southern Sunrise"
     Christian Science Monitor, 26 August 1959, 8
     Fiesta Melons (1971)

227 "Sow"
     Poetry, 90 (July 1957), 231-233
     The Colossus (1960)
     Tri-Quarterly, 7 (Fall 1966), 11-13

228 "Spider"
     Pursuit (1973)

229 "Spinster"
     Smith Alumnae Quarterly, 49 (Winter 1958), 71
     London Magazine, 5 (June 1958), 46-47
     The Colossus (1960)

230   "Stars over the Dordogne"
      Poetry, 99 (March 1962), 346-347

231   "Stillborn"
      The New Statesman, 81 (19 March 1971), 384
      Mademoiselle, 73 (September 1971), 161
      Crossing the Water (1971)

232   "Stings" [1]
      London Magazine, New Series 3 (April 1963), 26-27
      Ariel (1965)
      Tri-Quarterly, 7 (Fall 1966), 24-25
      Naked Poetry (1969)

233   "Stings" [2]
      Pursuit (1973)

234   "The Stones" (part VII of "Poem for a Birthday")
      The Colossus (1960)
      Contemporary American Poetry (1975)

235   "Stopped Dead"
      London Magazine, New Series 2 (January 1963), 14-
      15
      Crystal Gazer (1971)
      Winter Trees (1971)
      Mademoiselle, 74 (March 1972), 30

236   "Street Song"
      Cambridge Review, 90 (7 February 1969), 244

237   "Strumpet Song"
      Poetry, 89 (January 1957), 233
      The Colossus (1960)

238   "Suicide off Egg Rock"
      Hudson Review, 13 (Autumn 1960), 415
      The Colossus (1960)
      The New Poetry (1967)
      Possibilities of Poetry (1970)

239   "The Suitcases Are Packed Again"
      Seventeen, 12 (March 1953)

240   "The Surgeon at 2 a.m."
      The Listener, 68 (20 September 1962), 428
      Mademoiselle, 73 (September 1971), 160-161

Fiesta Melons (1971)
Crossing the Water (1971)

241 "The Swarm"
Encounter, 21 (October 1963), 45-46
Ariel (American editions only, 1966)
Winter Trees (British edition only, 1971)

242 "Temper of Time"
The Nation, 181 (6 August 1955), 119
Pursuit (1973)

243 "Thalidomide" (also see "Half Moon")
Encounter, 21 (October 1963), 51
The Art of Sylvia Plath (1970), 273-279
Winter Trees (1971)

244 "The Thin People"
London Magazine, 6 (October 1959), 12-13
The Colossus (1960)

245 "Three Women: A Poem for Three Voices"
Three Women (1968)
Critical Quarterly, 10 (Autumn 1968), 213-214.
Excerpt.
Transatlantic Review, 31 (Winter 1968/69), 51-52.
Excerpt.
Quarterly Review of Literature, 16 (1969), 197-198.
Excerpt.
The Art of Sylvia Plath (1970), 261-265. Excerpt.
Winter Trees (1971)
Ms., 1 (Spring 1972), 85-88. Excerpt.
Quarterly Review of Literature, 19 (1974), 447-448.
Excerpt.

246 "The Times Are Tidy"
Mademoiselle, 48 (January 1959), 34
The Colossus (1960)

247 "Tinker Jack and the Tidy Wives"
Accent, 17 (Autumn 1957), 248
Lyonnesse (1971)

248 "To Eva Descending the Stair"
Smith Review, Spring 1953, 22
Harper's, 209 (September 1954), 63

249 "Totem"
       New York Review of Books, 2 (20 February 1964),
         13
       Ariel (1965)

250 "The Tour"
       Times Literary Supplement, 28 May 1971, 610
       Crossing the Water (British edition only, 1971)
       Winter Trees (American edition only, 1972)

251 "Tulips"
       The New Yorker, 38 (7 April 1962), 40
       Ariel (1965)
       Poetry (1968)
       Naked Poetry (1969)
       Possibilities of Poetry (1970)
       Psyche (1973)
       The New Yorker Book of Poems (1974)
       The Norton Anthology of Poetry (Revised, 1975)

252 "Twelfth Night"
       Seventeen, 11 (December 1952)

253 "Two Campers in Cloud Country"
       The New Yorker, 39 (3 August 1963), 28
       Critical Quarterly, 12 (Summer 1970), 149
       Lyonnesse (1971)
       Crossing the Water (1971)
       The New Yorker Book of Poems (1974)

254 "Two Lovers and a Beachcomber by the Real Sea"
       Mademoiselle, 41 (August 1955), 52 and 62
       Granta, 61 (9 March 1957), 5
       Fiesta Melons (1971)

255 "Two Sisters of Persephone"
       Poetry, 89 (January 1957), 235-236
       The Colossus (British editions only, 1960)
       Crossing the Water (American editions only, 1971)

256 "Two Views of a Cadaver Room"
     . Times Literary Supplement, 6 November 1959,
         xxiii
       The Nation, 190 (30 January 1960), 107
       The Golden Year (1960)
       The Colossus (1960)
       The New Poetry (1967)

257 "Vanity Fair"
     Gemini, 1 (Spring 1957)

258 "Warning" (also see "Admonition")
     Harvard Advocate, 101 (May 1967), 2-3

259 "Watercolor of Grantchester Meadows"
     The New Yorker, 36 (28 May 1960), 30
     The Colossus (1960)
     Tri-Quarterly, 7 (Fall 1966), 13-14
     The New Yorker Book of Poems (1974)

260 "White Phlox"
     Christian Science Monitor, 27 August 1952, 12

261 "Whiteness I Remember"
     Christian Science Monitor, 5 March 1959, 12.

262 "Whitsun"
     London Magazine, New Series 1 (August 1961), 9
     Crossing the Water (1971)

263 "Who" (part I of "Poem for a Birthday")
     The Colossus (British editions only, 1960)
     Crossing the Water (American editions only, 1971)

264 "Widow"
     Poetry, 99 (March 1962), 347-348
     Lyonnesse (1971)
     Crossing the Water (1971)

265 "A Winter Ship"
     Atlantic, 206 (July 1960), 65
     A Winter Ship (1960)
     The Colossus (1960)
     Encounter, 16 (February 1961), 23

266 "Winter Trees"
     The Observer, 13 January 1963, 22
     Winter Trees (1971)
     Mademoiselle, 74 (March 1972), 30
     Contemporary American Poetry (1975)

267 "Wintering"
     Atlantic, 211 (April 1963), 70-71
     Ariel (1965)

268 "A Winter's Tale"
     The New Yorker, 35 (12 December 1959), 116
     Lyonnesse (1971)

269   "Witch Burning" (part VI of "Poem for a Birthday")
      Texas Quarterly, 4 (Autumn 1961), 84
      The Colossus (British editions only, 1960)
      Crossing the Water (American editions only, 1971)

270   "Words"
      Ariel (1965)
      Tri-Quarterly, 7 (Fall 1966), 38

271   "Words for a Nursery"
      Atlantic, 208 (August 1961), 66
      Tri-Quarterly, 7 (Fall 1966), 21-22
      The Art of Sylvia Plath (1970), 248-249

272   "Words Heard, by Accident, over the Phone"
      Pursuit (1973)

273   "Wreath for a Bridal"
      Poetry, 89 (January 1957), 231
      Wreath for a Bridal (1970)
      Lyonnesse (1971)

274   "Wuthering Heights"
      The New Statesman, 63 (16 March 1962), 390
      Uncollected Poems (1965)
      Crossing the Water (1971)

275   "Yadwigha, on a Red Couch, Among Lilies (A Sestina
      for the Douanier)"
      Christian Science Monitor, 26 March 1959, 8
      Fiesta Melons (1971)
      Crystal Gazer (1971)

276   "Years"
      London Magazine, New Series 3 (April 1963), 32
      Ariel (1965)

277   "You're"
      Harper's, 222 (June 1961), 40
      London Magazine, New Series 1 (August 1961), 6
      Ariel (1965)

278   "Zoo Keeper's Wife"
      London Magazine, New Series 1 (August 1961), 5-6
      Crystal Gazer (1971)
      Crossing the Water (1971)

C. PUBLISHED PROSE

279 "All the Dead Dears"
      Gemini, 1 (Summer 1957), 53-59
      Johnny Panic and the Bible of Dreams (1977)

280 "America! America!"
      Punch, 244 (3 April 1963), 482-484
      Johnny Panic and the Bible of Dreams (1977)

281 "An American in Paris"
      Varsity, 21 April 1956

282 "And Summer Will Not Come Again"
      Seventeen, 9 (August 1950), 191, 275-276

283 "As a Baby-Sitter Sees It"
      Christian Science Monitor, 6 November 1951, 19,
          and 7 November 1951, 21

284 "B. and K. at the Claridge"
      Smith Alumnae Quarterly, 48 (Fall 1956), 16-17

285 "Beach Plum Season on Cape Cod"
      Christian Science Monitor, 14 August 1958, 17

286 "Cambridge Notes"
      Johnny Panic and the Bible of Dreams (1977)

287 "Charlie Pollard and the Beekeepers"
      Johnny Panic and the Bible of Dreams (1977)

288 "A Comparison"
      Johnny Panic and the Bible of Dreams (1977)

289 "Context"
      London Magazine, New Series 1 (February 1962),
          45-46

Johnny Panic and the Bible of Dreams (1977)

290 "The Daughters of Blossom Street"
     London Magazine, 7 (May 1960), 34-48
     Johnny Panic and the Bible of Dreams (1977)

291 "The Day Mr. Prescott Died"
     Granta, 60 (20 October 1956), 20-23
     Spare Rib, June 1973
     Johnny Panic and the Bible of Dreams (1977)

292 "Day of Success"
     Johnny Panic and the Bible of Dreams (1977)

293 "Eccentricity"
     The Listener, 79 (9 May 1968), 607

294 "Explorations Lead to Interesting Discoveries"
     Christian Science Monitor, 19 October 1959, 17

295 "The Fifteen-Dollar Eagle"
     Sewanee Review, 68 (October-December 1960), 603-
          618
     Penguin Modern Stories 2, ed. Judith Burnley.
       Harmondsworth, England: Penguin, 1969
     Johnny Panic and the Bible of Dreams (1977)

290 "The Fifty-Ninth Bear"
     London Magazine, 8 (February 1961), 11-20
     Works in Progress, ed. Martha Saxton. New York:
       Literary Guild, 1971
     Johnny Panic and the Bible of Dreams (1977)

297 "In the Mountains"
     Smith Review, Fall 1954, 2-5
     Johnny Panic and the Bible of Dreams (1977)

298 "Initiation"
     Seventeen, 12 (January 1953), 65, 92-94
     Johnny Panic and the Bible of Dreams (1977)

299 "Johnny Panic and the Bible of Dreams"
     Atlantic, 222 (September 1968), 54-60
     Best American Short Stories, ed. Foley and Burnett.
       Boston: Houghton-Mifflin, 1969
     The Naked i, ed. Frederick Karl and Leo Hamalian.
       New York: Fawcett, 1971
     Johnny Panic and the Bible of Dreams (1977)

300 "Kitchen of the Fig Tree"
     Christian Science Monitor, 5 May 1959, 8

301 "Leaves from a Cambridge Notebook"
     Christian Science Monitor, 5 March 1956, 17, and
     6 March 1956, 15.

302 "Mademoiselle's Last Word on College, '53"
     Mademoiselle, 37 (August 1953), 235

303 "Mosaics--An Afternoon of Discovery"
     Christian Science Monitor, 12 October 1959, 15

304 "Mothers"
     Johnny Panic and the Bible of Dreams (1977)

305 "The Mother's Union"
     McCall's, 100 (October 1972), 80-81, 126, 128,
     130, 142

306 "Oblongs"
     The New Statesman, 63 (18 May 1962), 724   [Re-
     view of The Emperor's Oblong Pancakes, by
     Peter Hughes, The Three Rebels, by Tomi Un-
     gerer, The Funny Thing, by Wanda Gag, and
     Dr. Spock Talks to Mothers]

307 "Ocean 1212-W"
     The Listener, 70 (29 August 1963), 312-313
     Writers on Themselves, introd. Herbert Read.
          London: BBC, 1964
     The Art of Sylvia Plath (1970)
     Johnny Panic and the Bible of Dreams (1977)

308 "Oregonian Original"
     The New Statesman, 63 (9 November 1962), 660
          [Review of four children's books]

309 "Pair of Queens"
     The New Statesman, 63 (27 April 1962), 602-603
          [Review of A Queen of Spain, by Peter de Poinay,
     and Josephine, by Hubert Cole]

310 "The Perfect Setup"
     Seventeen, 11 (August 1952), 76, 100-104

311 "Poets on Campus"
     Mademoiselle, 37 (August 1953), 290-291 [Inter-

views with Anthony Hecht, Alastair Reid, Richard
Wilbur, George Steiner, and William Burford]

312 "Rose and Percy Key"
     Johnny Panic and the Bible of Dreams (1977)

313 "Sketchbook of a Spanish Summer"
     Christian Science Monitor, 5 November 1956, 13
         and 6 November 1956, 15 [with four drawings by
         Sylvia Plath]

314 "Smith College in Retrospect"
     Varsity, 12 May 1956

315 "Smith Review Revived"
     Smith Alumnae Quarterly, 45 (Fall 1953), 26

316 "Snow Blitz"
     Johnny Panic and the Bible of Dreams (1977)

317 "Suffering Angel"
     The New Statesman, 63 (7 December 1962), 828-
         829 [Review of Lord Byron's Wife, by Malcolm
         Elwin.]

318 "Sunday at the Mintons'"
     Mademoiselle, 35 (August 1952), 255, 371 370
     Smith Review, Fall 1952, 3-9
     Johnny Panic and the Bible of Dreams (1977)

319 "Superman and Paula Brown's New Snowsuit"
     Smith Review, Spring 1955, 19-21
     Johnny Panic and the Bible of Dreams (1977)

320 "Sylvia Plath Tours the Stores and Forecasts May Week
     Fashions"
     Varsity, 26 May 1956

321 "A Walk to Withens"
     Christian Science Monitor, 6 June 1959, 12

322 "What I Found Out About Buddy Willard"
     McCall's, 98 (April 1971), 86-87 [excerpt from The
         Bell Jar]

323 "Widow Mangada"
     Johnny Panic and the Bible of Dreams (1977)

324 "The Wishing Box"
     Granta, 61 (26 January 1957), 3-5
     Atlantic, 214 (October 1964), 86-89
     Johnny Panic and the Bible of Dreams (1977)

325 "Youth's Plea for World Peace," with Perry Norton
     Christian Science Monitor, 16 March 1950, 19

D. UNPUBLISHED POEMS AND PROSE

(Prose pieces are indicated by an asterisk.)

326 "Adolescence"

327 "Advice for an Artificer"

328 "All I Can Tell You Is About the Fog"

329 "Alone and Alone in the Woods Was I"

330 "Among the tall deep-rooted grasses"

331 "Apology to an April Satyr" (also called "Apology to Pan")

332 "Apology to Pan" (also called "Apology to an April Satyr")

333 "Apparel for April"

334 "Apple Blossoms"

335 "April"

336 "April Aubade"

337 "April 18"

338 "April, 1948"

339 "Aquatic Nocturne"

340 "august night"

341 "Autumn Portrait"

342 "A Ballad"

367 "Desert Song" (also called "Desert Love Song")

368 "The Desperate Hours"

369 "Dialogue over a Ouija Board"

370 "Dirge"

371 "Dirge for Abigail" (also called "Dirge for a Maiden Aunt")

372 "Dirge for a Joker"

373 "Dirge for a Maiden Aunt" (also called "Dirge for Abigail")

374 "Dirge in Three Parts"

375 "The Dispossessed"

376 "Doom of Exiles"

377 "The Dream"

378 "Dreams"

379 "The Dying Witch Addresses Her Young Apprentice"

380 "The earth had wilted in the heat"

381 "Earthbound"

382 "Elegy"

383 "Elizabeth" (also called "Elizabeth in April")

384 "Elizabeth in April" (also called "Elizabeth")

385 "Enchantment"

386 "Ennui" [1]

387 "Ennui" [2]

388 "Epitaph in Three Parts"

389 "Eve Describes Her Birthday Party"

414   "I put my fingers in my ears"

415   "I Reach Out"

416   "I Thought That I Could Not Be Hurt"

417   "Ice Age" [1]

418   "Ice Age" [2]

419   "The Ideal"

420   "In the Corner of My Garden"

421   "In Memoriam"

422   "In Passing"

423   "Incident"

424   "Insolent Storm Strikes at the Skull"

425   "Interlude" (also called "May")

426   "The Invalid"

427   "Item: Stolen, One Suitcase"

428   "Jilted"

429   "Joy"

430   "Kitchen Interlude"

431   "Latvian Lament" (also called "Latvian Threnody" and
      "Seek No More the Young")

432   "Latvian Threnody" (also called "Latvian Lament" and
      "Seek No More the Young")

433   "Let the Rain Fall Gently"

434   "Lonely Song"

435   "Love Is a Parallax"

436   "Mad Maudlin" (also see the published poem ("Maudlin")

437 *"The Magic Mirror: A Study of the Double in Two of
     Dostoevsky's Novels" (undergraduate honors thesis,
     Smith College, 1955)

438 "March"

439 "March 15 Muse"

440 "March 21"

441 "marcia"

442 "May" (also called "Interlude")

443 "Midnight Snow"

444 "Mid-summer Mobile" (also called "Suspend This Day")

445 "Missing Mother"

446 "The Mistake"

447 "Monologue at 3 a.m." (also see the published poem
     "The Surgeon at 2 a.m. ")

448 "Moonsong at Morning"

449 *"A Morning in the Agora"

450 "Morning in the Hospital Solarium"

451 "Mornings of Mist"

452 "Motherly Love"

453 "Neither Moonlight Nor Starlight"

454 "Never Try to Know More Than You Should"

455 "Never Try to Trick Me with a Kiss"

456 "neveryou"

457 "New England Library"

458 "New England Winter without Snow"

459 "Nostalgia" (also called "Reverie")

460 "Not Here"

461 "Notes to a Neophyte"

462 "Obsession"

463 "October"

464 "Ode for Ted"

465 "On the Futility of a Lexicon"

466 "On Looking into the Eyes of a Demon Lover"

467 "P. N."

468 "Pagan Song"

469 "Paradox"

470 "Parallax"

471 "Patience"

472 "Pearls of Dew"

473 "A Peripatetic Sonnet" (also see the published poem "The Suitcases Are Packed Again")

474 "Persecuted"

475 "Perseus: The Triumph of Wit over Suffering"

476 "Pigeon Post"

477 "Plant a little seedling"

478 "Poem"

479 "Portrait"

480 "Portrait d'une Jeune Fille"

481 "The Princess and the Goblins"

482 "Question"

483 "Rain"

484 "Recognition"

485 "Reflection"

486 "Reverie" (also called "Nostalgia")

487 "Riddle"

488 "rondeau"

489 "Rondeau Redoublé"

490 "The Scarlet Beacon"

491 "The Scullion's Dream" (also called "Triolet Frivole")

492 "Sea Symphony"

493 "Seek No More the Young" (also called "Latvian Lament" and "Latvian Threnody")

494 *"The Shadow Girl"

495 "Silver Thread"

496 "Slow, slow, the rhythm of the moon"

497 *"A Smokey Blue Piano"

498 "The Snowflake Star"

499 "Solo"

500 "Song" [1]

501 "Song" [2]

502 "Song for a Thaw"

503 "Song of Eve"

504 "Song of the Daydreamer"

505 "Song of a Superfluous Spring"

506 "Song of the Wild Geese" (also called "Wild Geese")

507 "Sonnet" (also called "To Eva")

508   "Sonnet for a Green-Eyed Sailor"

509   "Sonnet to Satan"

510   "Sonnet to a Shade"

511   "A Sorcerer Bids Farewell to Seem"

512   "Sorrow"

513   "Spinning Song"

514   "Spring Again"

515   "The Spring Parade"

516   "Spring Sacrament"

517   "Spring Song"

518   "Spring Song to a Housewife"

519   "Steely-Blue Crags"

520   "The Stoic"

521   "The Stranger"

522   "The stream, from a subterranean"

523   "Summer Street"

524   "Suspend This Day" (also called "Mid-summer Mobile")

525   "Swords into Plowshares" (also see the published poem "Bitter Strawberries")

526   "Terminal"

527   "Thoughts"

528   "Thy Kingdom Come"

529   "To Ariadne (deserted by Theseus)"

530   "To the Boy Inscrutable as God"

531   "To a Dissembling Spring"

532 "To Eva" (also called "Sonnet")

533 "To a Jilted Lover"

534 "To Time"

535 "Torch Song"

536 "Touch and Go"

537 "The Traveller"

538 "The Trial of Man"

539 "Triolet Frivole" [1]

540 "Triolet Frivole" [2] (also called "The Scullion's Dream")

541 "Tulips at Dawn"

542 "Twilight"

543 "Valentine; Lines to a Rich Bachelor"

544 "Van Winkle's Village"

545 "Verbal Calisthenics"

546 *"Victory"

547 "Virus TV (or We Don't Have a Set Either)"

548 "Voices"

549 "Wallflower"

550 "Wayfaring at the Whitney"

551 "Wellfleet Beach Plums"

552 "When the Stars Are Pale and Cool"

553 "White Girl between Yellow Curtains"

554 "Why must the slim spring rains fall now"

555 "Wild Geese" (also called "Song of the Wild Geese")

556 "A Winter Sunset"

557 "Winter Words"

558 "A Wish upon a Star"

559 "Words of Advice to an English Prof"

560 "You have to have my fairy ears"

561 "Youth"

562 "Zeitgeist at the Zoo"

E. INTERVIEWS

563 "Four Young Poets." Mademoiselle, 48 (January 1959),
    34-35, 85. Interviewed by Corinne Robins.

564 "Sylvia Plath." In The Poet Speaks, ed. Peter Orr
    (London: Routledge & Kegan Paul, 1966; New York:
    Barnes & Noble, 1966), 167-172. Interview of 30
    October 1962.

565 [Sylvia Plath: A Reading and an Interview.] Recorded
    at Springfield, Massachusetts, 18 April 1958.
    Washington: Library of Congress, 1958.

566 "Two of a Kind." BBC: Poets in Partnership. Broad-
    cast 31 January 1961. Joint interview with Ted
    Hughes.

567 "Two of a Kind." BBC: Poets in Partnership. Broad-
    cast 19 March 1961. Continuation of the joint in-
    terview with Ted Hughes.

F. LETTERS

568 Letters Home: Correspondence 1950-1963, edited and
with commentary by Aurelia Schober Plath. New
York: Harper and Row, 1975; New York: Bantam,
1977 (paperback).

569 "Sylvia Plath on Her Love and Marriage."
Mademoiselle, 81 (July 1975), 82-87. Excerpts
from Letters Home.

570 Unpublished letters in the Plath Manuscript Collection
of the Lilly Library, Indiana University. See entry
under "G. Manuscripts" for a guide to this exten-
sive collection of letters both by and to Plath.

G. MANUSCRIPTS

With the exception of the materials indicated be-
low, Sylvia Plath's manuscripts remain in the
possession of the executrix of her estate, Olwyn
Hughes. They are at present unavailable to
scholars. The holdings consist of holographic
worksheets and typewritten drafts of the late
poems--in some cases as many as ten sheets per
poem--and of typewritten versions of the earlier
poems. There are also notebooks, journals, and
other materials. Olwyn and Ted Hughes are
presently considering sale of the manuscripts to
a major library, but when such a sale will be
completed and the material made available is uncertain.

571 Cambridge Manuscript. English Faculty Library, Cam-
     bridge. Submitted by Sylvia Plath toward Part
     Two of the English Tripos in 1957. Contents:
          Wreath for a Bridal
          Monologue at 3 a. m.
          Street Song
          Strumpet Song
          Letter to a Purist
          The Glutton
          The Shrike
          Two Sisters of Persephone
          Spinster
          Ella Mason and Her Eleven Cats
          Miss Drake Proceeds to Supper
          Vanity Fair
          To Eva Descending the Stair
          Tinker Jack and the Tidy Wives
          The Snowman on the Moor
          Apotheosis
          Complaint of the Crazed Queen
          Mad Girl's Love Song
          Pursuit

Recantation
Mad Maudlin
Epitaph for Fire and Flower
Metamorphosis
Go Get the Goodly Squab
Sow
Touch and Go
On the Plethora of Dryads
Soliloquy of the Solipsist
On the Difficulty of Conjuring Up a Dryad
Two Lovers and a Beachcomber by the Real Sea
Resolve
Natural History
Dream of the Hearse-Driver
Aerialist
Dream with Clam Diggers
Pigeon Post
Black Rook in Rainy Weather
Lament
November Graveyard
Temper of Time
The Lady and the Earthenware Head
All the Dead Dears
Doomsday

572 "Thalidomide." Holographic worksheets and typewritten
     drafts. Printed in The Art of Sylvia Plath, ed.
     Charles Newman (Bloomington: Indiana University
     Press, 1070, London: Faber & Faber, 1970),
     273-279.

573 Lilly Library Collection. Lilly Library, Indiana Uni-
     versity, Bloomington. Purchased from Aurelia
     Plath, March 1977. The collection consists of cor-
     respondence both to and from Sylvia Plath, her
     writings, and memorabilia. Included are the orig-
     inal typescript of Letters Home--substantially dif-
     ferent from the published version--some two-hun-
     dred poems, sixty works of fiction, and fifteen
     pieces of non-fiction. Much of this material is un-
     published. Correspondents include Elizabeth Bowen,
     Peter Davison, Paul Hamilton Engle, Ted Hughes,
     Lynne Lawner, Russell Lynes, Olive Higgins Prou-
     ty, Henry Rago, Bryna Ivens Untermeyer, Edward
     Augustus Weeks, William Carlos Williams, and
     many others. Memorabilia run the range of a ba-
     by book, Smith College papers, artwork, swatches

of hair, photographs, and scrapbooks. A catalog
of the holdings is available from the Manuscripts
Department of the Lilly Library.

H. DRAWINGS

574 [Three Drawings.] "Wuthering Heights," "Benidorm," and
"Rock Harbour, Cape Cod. " In The Art of Sylvia
Plath, ed. Charles Newman (Bloomington: Indiana
University Press, 1970; London: Faber and Faber,
1970), 280-282.

575 [Eight Drawings.] In The Bell Jar (American editions
only, 1971).

576 [Frontispiece Drawing.] In Crystal Gazer (1971).

577 [Eleven Drawings.] In Fiesta Melons (1971).

578 [Four Drawings.] "Sardine boats and lights patterned
the beach during the daylight hours"; "At sunup,
the banana stand at the peasant market at Benidorm
opened for business"; "Palms and pueblos on the
sea cliffs at Benidorm, Spain"; and "Arched stair-
way to Castillo, in Benidorm. " Accompanying
"Sketchbook of a Spanish Summer. " Christian
Science Monitor, 5 November 1956, 13, and 6 November 1956, 15.

579 [Jacket Drawing.] "Wuthering Heights. " In Uncollected
Poems (1965).

580 Unpublished drawings in the Plath Manuscript Collection
of the Lilly Library, Indiana University. See entry
under "G. Manuscripts" for a guide to this collection.

I. RECORDINGS

581 "Contemporary American Poetry." BBC: New Comment. Broadcast 10 January 1963. Sylvia Plath reviews Donald Hall's anthology.

582 "In a World of Sound: What You Value Stays." BBC. Broadcast 7 September 1962.

583 "New Poetry." BBC: Third Programme. Broadcast 20 November 1960. Sylvia Plath reads "Candles" and "Leaving Early."

584 The Poet Speaks, ed. Peter Orr. Volume 5 (Argo PLP 1085). Sylvia Plath reads "Daddy," "Fever 103°," and "Lady Lazarus." Also comments from a BBC interview. London: Argo Record Company, 1965.

585 "A Poet's View of Novel Writing." BBC: The World of Books. Broadcast 7 July 1962.

586 "The Poet's Voice." BBC: Third Programme. Broadcast 24 August 1962. Sylvia Plath reads "The Surgeon at 2 a.m."

587 Spoken Arts Treasury of 100 Modern Poets Reading Their Poems. Volume 18 (Spoken Arts 1057). Sylvia Plath reads "The Applicant," Lady Lazarus," "Medusa," and "Stopped Dead."

588 [Sylvia Plath: A Reading and an Interview.] Recorded at Springfield, Massachusetts, 18 April 1958. Washington: Library of Congress, 1958.

589 Sylvia Plath Reads Plath. An interview with Peter Orr and a reading. Credo records, 3, 1975. Sylvia Plath reads "Lady Lazarus," "Stopped Dead," "Nick and the Candlestick," "Medusa," "Purdah,"

"Amnesiac, " "Fever 103°, " "The Rabbit Catcher, "
"Ariel, " "Poppies in October, " "The Applicant, "
"A Secret, " "Cut, " "A Birthday Present, " and
"Daddy. " Recorded 30 October 1962.

590 "Two of a Kind. " BBC: Poets in Partnership. Broadcast 31 January 1961. Joint interview with Ted
Hughes.

591 "Two of a Kind. " BBC: Poets in Partnership. Broadcast 19 March 1961. Continuation of the joint interview with Ted Hughes.

592 Writers on Themselves. BBC. Broadcast 19 August
1963. Sylvia Plath reads "Ocean 1212-W. "

J. WORK EDITED

593 American Poetry Now: Critical Quarterly Supplement
Number Two, ed. Sylvia Plath. London: Oxford University Press, 1961.

K. TRANSLATIONS

594 "The Applicant":
   "Le Candidat, " trans. Raymond Federman.
   "Poèmes par Sylvia Plath. " Esprit, 371 (May
   1968), 829-830. French.

595 Ariel:
   Eariaru, trans. Tokunaga Shozo. Tokyo: Kozosha,
   1971. Japanese.
   Mittokh Rimze Ha-Efer, trans. M. Ovadyahu. Tel-
   Aviv: Gallim, 1965. Hebrew.

596 The Bell Jar:
   La campana de cristal, trans. Myrian McGee.
   Caracas: Editorial Tiempo Nuevo, 1971.
   Spanish.
   La campana di vetro, trans. Daria Menicanti. Mi-
   lano: Mondadori, 1968. Italian.
   Die Glasglocke, trans. Christian Grote. Frankfurt
   am Main: Suhrkamp, 1968. German

597 "Childless Woman":
   "Sans enfant, " trans. Raymond Federman.
   "Poèmes par Sylvia Plath. " Esprit, 371 (May
   1968), 831. French.

598 "Contusion":
   "Contusion, " trans. Raymond Federman.
   "Poèmes par Sylvia Plath. " Esprit, 371 (May
   1968), 832. French.

599 "Daddy":
   "Pappa, " trans. Raymond Federman. "Poèmes
   par Sylvia Plath. " Esprit, 371 (May 1968),
   825-827. French.

600 "The Hanging Man":
   "Le Pendu, " trans. Raymond Federman.

"Poèmes par Sylvia Plath." <u>Esprit</u>, 371 (May 1968), 828. French.

L.   DRAMATIC PERFORMANCES

601   "Sylvia Plath. "   Brooklyn Academy of Music, January
1974.
Plath's words from interviews, letters, and
works, with linking narrative from A. Alvarez's
The Savage God.
Also, her "Three Women," performed by the
Royal Shakespeare Repertory Theater Group, with
Brenda Bruce, Estelle Kohler, and Louise Jame-
son.

602   "Three Women: A Monologue for Three Voices. "
BBC: Third Programme.   Broadcast 19 August
1962.   Produced by Douglas Cleverdon.
"Wife":   Penelope Lee; "Secretary":   Jill Bal-
con; "Girl":   Janette Richter.

II

WORKS ABOUT SYLVIA PLATH

A. BOOKS
(with a selection of some reviews of them)

603 Aird, Eileen. Sylvia Plath: Her Life and Work.
Edinburgh: Oliver and Boyd, 1973; New York:
Barnes & Noble, 1973; New York: Harper & Row,
1975; New York: Harper & Row, 1975 (paperback).
[Also see Aird's thesis, item 1010.]

Booklist, 70 (1 January 1974), 469.
Choice, 11 (April 1974), 255.
Library Journal, 98 (1 November 1973), 3267.

604 Butscher, Edward. Sylvia Plath: Method and Madness.
New York: Seabury Press, 1976.

Booklist, 72 (1 February 1976), 746.
Kirkus Reviews, 43 (1 December 1975), 1358.
Maloff, Saul. Commonweal, 103 (4 June 1976),
371-374.
Perloff, Marjorie. "Breaking the Bell Jar."
Washington Post Book World, 4 April 1976, 1-2.
Sternman, William. Best Sellers, 36 (June 1976),
78-79.
Straus, Harriet. Library Journal, 101 (15 March
1976), 815.
"Sylvia Plath: Method and Madness." Publishers
Weekly, 209 (5 January 1976), 62.

605 Holbrook, David. Sylvia Plath: Poetry and Existence.
London: The Athlone Press, 1976.

606 Kroll, Judith. Chapters in a Mythology: The Poetry of
Sylvia Plath. New York: Harper & Row, 1976.
[Also see Kroll's dissertation, item 1018.]

67

607 Melander, Ingrid. The Poetry of Sylvia Plath: A Study
     of Themes. Stockholm: Almqvist & Wiksell, 1972
     (Gothenburg Studies in English No. 25).

608 Newman, Charles, ed. The Art of Sylvia Plath: A
     Symposium. Bloomington: Indiana University
     Press, 1970; London: Faber & Faber, 1970. Con-
     tents indexed separately under II.B., Articles
     about Sylvia Plath.

     Booklist, 66 (15 May 1970), 1134.
     Hedberg, Johannes. Moderna Språk, 64 (1970),
        83-86.
     Hughes, John W. "Insights and Oversights in the
        Poetic Vision." Saturday Review, 53 (8 August
        1970), 33-35.
     Manchester Guardian Weekly, 17 January 1970, 18.
     Milner, Ian. Philologica Pragensia, 13 (1970),
        220.
     Neiswender, Rosemary. "Commentaries on a Dark,
        Confessional Poet." Library Journal, 95 (15
        February 1970), 668.
     The Observer, 1 February 1970, 30.
     Porter, Peter. "Death as Key." The New States-
        man, 79 (9 January 1970), 52-53.
     Saal, Rollene W. "Pick of the Paperbacks." Sa-
        turday Review, 54 (27 November 1971), 48-49,
        91.
     Seymour-Smith, Martin. "Hard Truth." The Spec-
        tator, 224 (17 January 1970), 80.
     "Sylvia Plath: Cult and Backlash." Times Litera-
        ry Supplement, 12 February 1970, 151.

609 Steiner, Nancy Hunter. A Closer Look at Ariel: A
     Memory of Sylvia Plath. New York: Harper Maga-
     zine Press, 1973; New York: Popular Library
     Press, 1974 (paperback); London: Faber & Faber,
     1974; London: Faber & Faber, 1974 (paperback).
     All with an introduction by George Stade.

B. ARTICLES

610 Adrich, Elizabeth. "Sylvia Plath's 'The Eye-Mote': An Analysis. " Harvard Advocate, 101 (May 1967), 4-7.

611 Aird, Eileen M. "Variants in a Tape Recording of Fifteen Poems by Sylvia Plath. " Notes and Queries, 19 (February 1972), 59-61.

612 Alvarez, A. "The Art of Suicide. " Partisan Review, 37 (1970), 339-358.

613 _____. "Beyond All This Fiddle. " Times Literary Supplement, 23 March 1967, 229-232. Reprinted in Alvarez's Beyond All This Fiddle (New York: Random House, 1968), 3-21.

614 _____. [Letter to the Editor.] The Observer, 21 November 1971, 10. [Reply to Ted Hughes' letter (item 700) of the previous week.]

615 _____. "A Poet's Epitaph. " The Observer, 17 February 1963, 23.

616 _____. "Publish and Be Damned. " The Observer, 1 October 1971, 36.

617 _____. "Sylvia Plath. " B. B. C. Third Programme, 1963. First printed in The Review, 9 (October 1963), 20-26. Reprinted with some revision in Tri-Quarterly, 7 (Fall 1966), 65-74. Revised form reprinted in Alvarez's Beyond All This Fiddle (New York: Random House, 1968), 45-58. Same form reprinted in The Art of Sylvia Plath, ed. Charles Newman (Bloomington: Indiana University Press, 1970; London: Faber & Faber, 1970), 56-68.

618 _____. "Sylvia Plath: The Cambridge Collection. "

69

Cambridge Review, 90 (7 February 1969), 246-247.
Reprinted in The Cambridge Mind, ed. Eric Homberger et al. (Boston: Little, Brown, 1970), 299-
303.

619 _____. "Sylvia Plath: A Memoir." New American
Review, 12 (1971), 9-40. Reprinted in Intellectual
Digest, 2 (November 1971), 90-95. Reprinted in
Alvarez's The Savage God: A Study of Suicide
(London: Weidenfeld and Nicolson, 1971; New York:
Random House, 1972), 5-34.

620 _____. "Sylvia Plath: The Road to Suicide." The
Observer, 14 November 1971, 25. Excerpt from
Alvarez's The Savage God: A Study of Suicide
(London: Weidenfeld and Nicolson, 1971; New York:
Random House, 1972).

621 _____. Times Literary Supplement, 26 November
1971, 1478. [Reply to Ted Hughes' letter (item
698) of the previous week.]

622 Ames, Lois. "Notes Toward a Biography." Tri-Quarterly, 7 (Fall 1966), 95-107. Reprinted in The Art
of Sylvia Plath, ed. Charles Newman (Bloomington:
Indiana University Press, 1970; London: Faber &
Faber, 1970), 155-173.

623 _____. "Sylvia Plath: A Biographical Note." In the
American editions of Plath's The Bell Jar (New
York: Harper & Row, 1971; New York: Bantam,
1972 [paperback]).

624 Arb, Siv. "Dikter når förvånansvärt långt." Ord och
Bild, 83 (1974), 459-460.

625 Ashford, Deborah. "Sylvia Plath's Poetry: A Complex
of Irreconcilable Antagonisms." Concerning Poetry,
7, no. 1, 62-69.

626 Bagg, Robert. "The Rise of Lady Lazarus." Mosaic,
2 (Summer 1969), 9-36.

627 Baker, A. T. "Poetry Today: Low Profile, Flatted
Voices." Time, 98 (12 July 1971), 61, 65-68.

628 Balitas, Vincent D. "A Note on Sylvia Plath's 'The

Hanging Man.'" Notes and Queries, 22 (May 1975),
208. Also published in Bulletin of the New York
C. S. Lewis Society, 6, ix, 11.

629 _____. "On Becoming a Witch: A Reading of Sylvia
Plath's 'Witch Burning.'" Studies in the Humanities, 4 (February 1975), 27-30.

630 Ballif, Gene. "Facing the Worst: A View from Miner-
va's Buckler." Parnassus: Poetry in Review,
Fall/Winter 1975, 231-259.

631 Bedford, Jean. "Sylvia Plath and Suicide." The Digger
(Australia), November-December 1974, 9.

632 Bergonzi, Bernard. "Letter re: 'After the Tranquillized Fifties.'" Critical Quarterly, 6 (Autumn
1964), 277.

633 Bierman, Larry. "'The Vivid Tulips Eat My Oxygen':
An Essay on Sylvia Plath's 'Ariel.'" Windless Orchard, 4 (February 1971), 44-46.

634 Birstein, Ann. "The Sylvia Plath Cult." Vogue, 158
(1 October 1971), 176.

635 Blodgett, E. D. "Sylvia Plath: Another View." Mo
dern Poetry Studies, 2 (1971), 97-106.

636 Bondy, François. "Selbstmord als Siegel der Wahr-
heit?" Neue Deutsche Hefte, 20 (1973), 126-131.

637 Boyers, Robert. "Sylvia Plath: The Trepanned Vete-
ran." Centennial Review, 13 (Spring 1969), 138-
153.

638 Buell, Frederick. "Sylvia Plath's Traditionalism."
Boundary, 2 (Fall 1976), 195-211.

639 Burnham, Richard E. "Sylvia Plath's 'Lady Lazarus.'"
Contemporary Poetry, 1, ii (1973), 42-46.

640 "Cache of Verse." The Times [London], 27 December
1968, 8g. [Discovery of the Cambridge Manuscript.]

641 Campbell, Wendy. "Remembering Sylvia." Cambridge

Review, 90 (7 February 1969), 253-254. Reprinted
in The Art of Sylvia Plath, ed. Charles Newman
(Bloomington: Indiana University Press, 1970; London: Faber & Faber, 1970), 182-186.

642 Caraher, Brian. "The Problematic of Body and Language in Sylvia Plath's 'Tulips.'" Paunch, 42-43:
76-89.

643 Christiaen, Cris. "Poet on College Time." Mademoiselle, 41 (August 1955), 49, 52, 62.

644 Claire, William F. "That Rare, Random Descent: The
Poetry and Pathos of Sylvia Plath." Antioch Review, 26 (Winter 1966), 552-560.

645 Cleverdon, Douglas. "Preface." In Plath's Three
Women (London: Turret Books, 1966), 5-7. Re-
printed as "On Three Women" in The Art of Sylvia
Plath, ed. Charles Newman (Bloomington: Indiana
University Press, 1970; London: Faber & Faber,
1970), 227-229.

646 Cluysenaar, Anne. "Post-culture: Pre-culture?" In
British Poetry Since 1960: A Critical Survey, ed.
Michael Schmidt and Grevel Lindop (Oxford, Eng-
land: Carcanet Press, 1972), 215-232.

647 "A Conversation with Robert Lowell." The Review,
26 (Summer 1971), 10-29.

648 Cooley, Peter. "Autism, Autoeroticism, Auto-da-fe:
The Tragic Poetry of Sylvia Plath." Hollins Critic,
10 (February 1973), 1-15.

649 Corrigan, Sylvia Robinson. "Sylvia Plath: A New
Feminist Approach." Aphra, 1 (Spring 1970),
16-23.

650 Cox, C. B., and A. R. Jones. "After the Tranquillized Fifties: Notes on Sylvia Plath and James
Baldwin." Critical Quarterly, 6 (Summer 1964),
107-122. Partially reprinted as A. R. Jones' "On
'Daddy'" in The Art of Sylvia Plath, ed. Charles
Newman (Bloomington: Indiana University Press,
1970; London: Faber & Faber, 1970), 230-236.

651 Davis, Robin Reed. "The Honey Machine: Imagery
     Patterns in Ariel." New Laurel Review, 1 (Spring
     1972), 23-31.

652 _____. "Now I Have Lost Myself: A Reading of
     Sylvia Plath's 'Tulips.'" Paunch, 42-43: 97-104.

653 Davis, Stuart A. "The Documentary Sublime: The
     Posthumous Poetry of Sylvia Plath." Harvard Ad-
     vocate, 101 (May 1967), 8-12.

654 Davis, William V. "Sylvia Plath's 'Ariel.'" Modern
     Poetry Studies, 3 (1972), 176-184.

655 Dickey, James. "Spinning the Crystal Ball: Some
     Guesses at the Future of American Poetry." Li-
     brary of Congress Lecture, 24 April 1967 (Wash-
     ington D. C.: U. S. Government Printing Office, 1967).

656 Donovan, Josephine. "Sexual Politics in Sylvia Plath's
     Short Stories." Minnesota Review, 4 (Spring/Sum-
     mer 1973), 150-157.

657 Drexler, Rosalyn. "Her Poetry Is Her Triumph."
     New York Times (Sunday), 13 January 1974, Sec.
     2, 3. Reprinted in The New York Times, Bio-
     graphical Edition, 5 (January 1974), 106-107.

658 Duffy, Martha. "The Triumph of a Tormented Poet."
     Life, 71 (12 November 1971), 38a-38b. [Illustra-
     ted.]

659 Dunn, Douglas. "Damaged Instruments." Encounter
     37 (August 1971), 68-70.

660 _____. "Mechanics of Misery: Poetry Chronicle."
     Encounter, 41 (August 1973), 79-85.

661 Dyroff, Jan M. "Sylvia Plath: Perceptions in Crossing
     the Water." Art and Literature Review, 1, 49-50.

662 Dyson, A. E. "Sylvia Plath." Tri-Quarterly, 7 (Fall
     1966), 75-80. Reprinted as "On Sylvia Plath" in
     The Art of Sylvia Plath, ed. Charles Newman
     (Bloomington: Indiana University Press, 1970;
     London: Faber & Faber, 1970), 204-210.

663 Efron, Arthur. "Sylvia Plath's 'Tulips' and Literary
     Criticism. " Paunch, 42-43: 69-75.

664 _____. "'Tulips': Text and Assumptions. " Paunch,
     42-43: 110-122.

665 Ellmann, Mary. "The Bell Jar: An American Girl-
     hood. " In The Art of Sylvia Plath, ed. Charles
     Newman (Bloomington: Indiana University Press,
     1970; London: Faber & Faber, 1970), 221-226.

666 Eriksson, Pamela Dale. "Some Thoughts on Sylvia
     Plath. " Unisa English Studies, 10 (1972), 45-52.

667 Evans, Nancy Burr. "Looking Back Over Four Years. "
     College English, 35 (December 1973), 240-251.

668 Ferrier, Carole. "The Beekeeper and the Queen Bee. "
     Refractory Girl, Spring 1973, 31-36.

669 Frados, Julia Aldrich. "Letters: The Bell Jar. "
     New York Times Book Review, 20 June 1971, 34.

670 Fraser, G. S. "A Hard Nut to Crack from Sylvia
     Plath. " Contemporary Poetry, 1 (Spring 1973),
     1-12.

671 Gordon, Jan B. "'Who Is Sylvia?': The Art of Sylvia
     Plath. " Modern Poetry Studies, 1 (1970), 6-34.

672 Gustafson, Richard. "'Time Is a Waiting Woman':
     New Poetic Icons. " Midwest Quarterly, 16 (Spring
     1975), 318-327.

673 Guttman, Allen. "Love and Death and Dachau: Recent
     Poets. " Studies on the Left, 4 (Spring 1964), 98-
     109.

674 Hakeem, A. "Sylvia Plath's 'Elm' and Munch's 'The
     Scream. '" English Studies, 55 (December 1974),
     531-537.

675 Hardwick, Elizabeth. "Sylvia Plath. " New York Re-
     view of Books, 17 (12 August 1971), 3-4, 6. Re-
     printed as "On Sylvia Plath" in Poetry Dimension
     I: A Living Record of the Poetry Year, ed. Jere-
     my Robson (London: Robson Books, 1973), 13-29.

Also reprinted in Hardwick's Seduction and Betrayal:
Women and Literature (New York: Random House,
1974; London: Weidenfeld and Nicolson, 1974), 104-
121.

676   Hardy, Barbara.   "The Poetry of Sylvia Plath: Enlarge-
ment or Derangement?" In The Survival of Poetry:
A Contemporary Survey, ed. Martin Dodsworth
(London: Faber & Faber, 1970), 164-187.

677   Herzberg, Judith.   "De Moed der Wanhoop." Tirade,
9 (Summer 1965), 500-504.

678   Heseltine, H. P.   "Ripeness Is All: The Example of
Keats." Teaching of English, 20 (June 1971), 23-
37.

679   Himelick, Raymond.   "Notes on the Care and Feeding
of Nightmares: Burton, Erasmus, and Sylvia
Plath." Western Humanities Review, 28 (Autumn
1974), 313-326.

680   Hoffman, Nancy Jo.   "Reading Women's Poetry: The
Meaning and Our Lives." College English, 34 (October 1972), 48-62.

681   Holbrook, David.   "Out of the Ash: Different Views of
the 'Death Camp' Sylvia Plath, Al Alvarez, and
Viktor Frankl." The Human World, 5 (November
1971), 22-39.

682   _____.   "R. D. Laing and the Death Circuit." Encounter, 31 (August 1968), 35-45.

683   _____.   "Sylvia Plath--Pathological Morality and the
Avant-Garde." In Pelican Guide to English Litera-
ture: The Modern Age, Vol. 7, ed. Boris Ford
(Harmondsworth, England: Penguin Books, 1974).

684   _____.   "Sylvia Plath and the Problem of Violence
in Art." Cambridge Review, 90 (7 February 1969),
249-250.

685   _____.   "The 200-Inch Distorting Mirror." New Society, 12 (11 July 1968), 57-58.

686   Homberger, Eric.   "I Am I." Cambridge Review, 90
(7 February 1969), 251-252.

687 _____. "The Uncollected Plath." The New States-
        man, 22 September 1972, 404-405.

688 Horowitz, Israel. "'Some God Got Hold of Me.'" Vil-
        lage Voice, 28 October 1971, 27-30.

689 _____. "Success in Spite of Suicide." Village
        Voice, 4 November 1971, 27.

690 Hosbaum, Philip. "The Temptations of Giant Despair."
        Hudson Review, 25 (Winter 1972/73), 597-612.

691 Howard, Richard. "Sylvia Plath: 'And I Have No Face,
        I Have Wanted to Efface Myself....'" In The Art
        of Sylvia Plath, ed. Charles Newman (Bloomington:
        Indiana University Press, 1970; London: Faber &
        Faber, 1970), 77-88.   Reprinted, with slight re-
        vision, in Howard's Alone with America; Essays on
        the Art of Poetry in the United States Since 1950
        (New York: Atheneum, 1969), 413-422.

692 Howe, Irving. "Letters from Readers: Politics and
        Poetry." Commentary, 58 (October 1974), 9, 12.

693 _____. "The Plath Celebration: A Partial Dissent."
        In Howe's The Critical Point: On Literature and
        Culture (New York: Horizon Press, 1973), 158-
        169.

694 _____. "Sylvia Plath: A Partial Disagreement."
        Harper's, 244 (January 1972), 88-91.

695 Hoyle, James F. "Sylvia Plath: A Poetry of Suicidal
        Mania." Literature and Psychology, 18 (1968),
        187-203.

696 Hughes, Catharine. "Britain in Brooklyn: Royal Shake-
        speare Production Drawn from Works." America,
        130 (9 February 1974), 92.

697 Hughes, Olwyn. "To the Editor: The Savage God."
        Times Literary Supplement, 3 December 1971, 1525.
        [Letter concerning Alvarez's memoir and the Ted
        Hughes and A. Alvarez controversy over it.]

698 Hughes, Ted. "Commentary." Times Literary Supple-
        ment, 19 November 1971, 1448.   [Letter concerning
        the A. Alvarez memoir. (See also item 621.)]

699   _____ . "Notes on the Chronological Order of Sylvia
           Plath's Poems. " Tri-Quarterly, 7 (Fall 1966), 81-
           88. Reprinted in The Art of Sylvia Plath, ed.
           Charles Newman (Bloomington: Indiana University
           Press, 1970; London: Faber & Faber, 1970), 187-
           195.

700   _____ . "Sylvia Plath. " The Observer, 21 November
           1971, 10. [Letter concerning the A. Alvarez mem-
           oir. (See also item 614.)]

701   _____ . "Sylvia Plath. " Poetry Book Society Bulle-
           tin, 44 (February 1965).

702   _____ . "Sylvia Plath's Crossing the Water: Some
           Reflections. " Critical Quarterly, 13 (Summer
           1971), 165-172.

703   _____ . "Ten Poems by Sylvia Plath. " Encounter,
           21 (October 1963), 45.

704 Jennings, Carol. "The Woman Poet. " New York
           Quarterly, 12 (Autumn 1972), 123-126.

705 Jones, A. R. "Necessity and Freedom: The Poetry
           of Robert Lowell, Sylvia Plath, and Anne Sexton. "
           Critical Quarterly, 7 (Spring 1965), 11-30.

706   _____ . "On 'Daddy. '" In The Art of Sylvia Plath,
           ed. Charles Newman (Bloomington: Indiana Uni-
           versity Press, 1970; London: Faber & Faber,
           1970), 230-236.

707 Kalem, T. E. "Toppled King/Torn Mind. " Time,
           103 (28 January 1974), 77.

708 Kamel, Rose. "'A Self to Recover': Sylvia Plath's
           Bee Cycle Poems. " Modern Poetry Studies, 4
           (1973), 304-318.

709 Kell, Richard. "Letter re 'After the Tranquillized
           Fifties. '" Critical Quarterly, 6 (Autumn 1964),
           276.

710 Kissick, Gary. "Plath: A Terrible Perfection. " The
           Nation, 207 (16 September 1968), 245-247.

711   Klein, Elinor, "A Friend Recalls Sylvia Plath." Gla-
      mour, November 1966, 168, 182-184.

712   Lane, Gary. "Sylvia Plath's 'The Hanging Man': A
      Further Note." Contemporary Poetry, 2 (Spring
      1975), 40-43.

713   Lavers, Annette. "The World as Icon: On Sylvia
      Plath's Themes." In The Art of Sylvia Plath, ed.
      Charles Newman (Bloomington: Indiana University
      Press, 1970; London: Faber & Faber, 1970),
      100-135.

714   Libby, Anthony. "God's Lioness and the Priest of
      Sycorax: Plath and Hughes." Contemporary Litera-
      ture, 15 (Summer 1974), 386-405.

715   Lindberg-Seyersted, Brita. "Notes on Three Poems by
      Sylvia Plath." Edda, 74 (1974), 47-54.

716   _____. "On Sylvia Plath's Poetry." Edda, 72 (1972),
      54-59.

717   Locke, Richard. "The Last Word: Beside The Bell
      Jar." New York Times Book Review, 20 June
      1971, 47.

718   Lowell, Robert. "On Two Poets." New York Review
      of Books, 6 (12 May 1966), 3-4. Excerpted as
      "Foreword" in the American editions of Plath's
      Ariel (New York: Harper & Row, 1966).

719   Lucie-Smith, Edward. "A Murderous Art." Critical
      Quarterly, 6 (1964), 355-363.

720   _____. "Sea-Imagery in the Work of Sylvia Plath."
      In The Art of Sylvia Plath, ed. Charles Newman
      (Bloomington: Indiana University Press, 1970;
      London: Faber & Faber, 1970), 91-99.

721   McClatchy, J. D. "Staring from Her Hood of Bone:
      Adjusting to Sylvia Plath." In American Poetry
      Since 1960: Some Critical Perspectives, ed.
      Robert Burns Shaw (Oxford, England: Carcanet
      Press, 1973; Chester Springs, Pennsylvania: Du-
      four Editions, 1974), 155-166.

722 McKay, D. F. "Aspects of Energy in the Poetry of
     Dylan Thomas and Sylvia Plath. " Critical Quarter-
     ly, 16 (Spring 1974), 53-67.

723 Malkoff, Karl. "The Confessional Poets. " In Malkoff's
     Crowell's Handbook of Contemporary American
     Poetry (New York: Thomas Y. Crowell, 1973),
     25-35.

724 _____. "Sylvia Plath. " In Malkoff's Crowell's
     Handbook of Contemporary American Poetry (New
     York: Thomas Y. Crowell, 1973), 245-252.

725 Martin, Wendy. "'God's Lioness'--Sylvia Plath, Her
     Prose and Poetry. " Women's Studies, 1 (1973).
     191-198.

726 Marvel, Bill. "Unsung in Life, Lionized in Death. "
     National Observer, 12 (10 February 1973), 1, 18.

727 Megna, Jerome. "Plath's 'The Manor Garden.'" Ex-
     plicator, 30 (March 1972), Item 58.

728 Meissner, William. "The Opening of the Flower: The
     Revelation of Suffering in Sylvia Plath's 'Tulips.'"
     Contemporary Poetry, 1 (Spring 1973), 13-17.

729 _____. "The Rise of the Angel: Life Through Death
     in the Poetry of Sylvia Plath. " Massachusetts
     Studies in English, 3 (Fall 1971), 34-39.

730 Melander, Ingrid. "'The Disquieting Muses': A Note
     on a Poem by Sylvia Plath. " Research Studies
     (Washington State University), 39 (March 1971),
     53-54.

731 _____. "'Watercolour of Grantchester Meadows':
     An Early Poem by Sylvia Plath. " Moderna Språk,
     65 (1971), 1-5.

732 Milliner, Gladys W. "The Tragic Imperative: The
     Awakening and The Bell Jar. " Mary Wollstonecraft
     Newsletter, 2 (1973), 21-27.

733 Mizejewski, Linda. "Sappho to Sexton: Woman Uncon-
     tained. " College English, 35 (December 1973),
     340-345.

734 Mollinger, Robert N. "A Symbolic Complex: Images
     of Death and Daddy in the Poetry of Sylvia Plath. "
     Descant, 19, ii, 44-52.

735 _____. "Sylvia Plath's 'Private Ground. '" Notes on
     Contemporary Literature, 5, ii, 14-15.

736 Monteith, Charles. "To the Editor: The Bell Jar. "
     Times Literary Supplement, 7 December 1973,
     1508b.

737 Murdoch, Brian. "Transformations of the Holocaust:
     Auschwitz in Modern Lyric Poetry. " Comparative
     Literature Studies, 11 (June 1974), 123-150.

738 Murray, Michele. "Okay, Sylvia Plath Was Good, But
     Not That Good. " National Observer, 11 (30 Sep-
     tember 1972), 27.

739 Newlin, Margaret. "The Suicide Bandwagon. " Critical
     Quarterly, 14 (Winter 1972), 367-378.

740 Newman, Charles. "Candor Is the Only Wile: The Art
     of Sylvia Plath. " Tri-Quarterly, 7 (Fall 1966), 39-
     64. Reprinted in The Art of Sylvia Plath, ed.
     Charles Newman (Bloomington: Indiana University
     Press, 1970; London: Faber & Faber, 1970),
     21-55.

741 Nims, John Frederick. "The Poetry of Sylvia Plath:
     A Technical Analysis. " In The Art of Sylvia
     Plath, ed. Charles Newman (Bloomington: Indiana
     University Press, 1970; London: Faber & Faber,
     1970), 136-152.

742 Oates, Joyce Carol. "The Death Throes of Romantic-
     ism: The Poems of Sylvia Plath. " Southern Re-
     view, 9 (Summer 1973), 501-522. Reprinted in
     Contemporary Poetry in America: Essays and In-
     terviews, ed. Robert Boyers (New York: Schocken,
     1975), 139-156. Reprinted in Oates' New Heaven,
     New Earth: The Visionary Experience (New York:
     Vanguard, 1974), 111-140.

743 Oberg, Arthur K. "The Modern British and American
     Lyric: What Will Suffice?" Language and Litera-
     ture, 7 (Winter 1972), 70-88.

744 _____ . "Sylvia Plath and the New Decadence." Chi-
    cago Review, 20 (1968), 66-73.

745 The Observer. 21 November 1971, 10. [Editorial
    comment that Alvarez's memoir will not be con-
    tinued.]

746 Oettle, Pamela. "Sylvia Plath's Last Poems." Bal-
    cony, 3 (Spring 1965), 47-50.

747 Oliva, Renato. "La Poesia di Sylvia Plath." Studi
    Americani (Roma), 15 (1969), 341-381.

748 Oliver, Edith. "Off Broadway: Sylvia Plath." The
    New Yorker, 49 (28 January 1974), 69.

749 Oshio, Toshiko. "Sylvia Plath no Shi." Oberon, 14
    (1973), 45-59. [In Japanese.]

750 Ostriker, Alicia. "'Fact' as Style: The Americaniza-
    tion of Sylvia." Language and Style, 1 (Summer
    1968), 201-212.

751 Perloff, Marjorie. "Angst and Animism in the Poetry
    of Sylvia Plath." Journal of Modern Literature, 1
    (1970), 57-74.

752 _____ . "Extremist Poetry: Some Versions of the
    Sylvia Plath Myth." Journal of Modern Literature,
    2 (November 1972), 581-588.

753 _____ . "On Sylvia Plath's 'Tulips.'" Paunch, 42-43:
    105-109.

754 _____ . "On the Road to Ariel: The 'Transitional'
    Poetry of Sylvia Plath." Iowa Review, 4 (Spring
    1973), 94-110.

755 _____ . "'A Ritual for Being Born Twice': Sylvia
    Plath's The Bell Jar." Contemporary Literature,
    13 (Autumn 1972), 507-522.

756 Phillips, Robert. "The Dark Funnel: A Reading of
    Sylvia Plath." Modern Poetry Studies, 3 (1972),
    49-74. Reprinted in Phillips' The Confessional
    Poets (Carbondale: Southern Illinois University
    Press, 1973), 128-151.

757 Plath, Aurelia Schober, and Robert Robinson. "Sylvia
     Plath's Letters Home: Some Reflections by Her
     Mother." The Listener, 95 (22 April 1976), 515-
     516.

758 Poulin, H., Jr. "Contemporary American Poetry: The
     Radical Tradition." Concerning Poetry, 3 (Fall
     1970), 5-21.

759 Pratt, Linda Ray. "'The Spirit of Blackness Is in
     Us....'" Prairie Schooner, 47 (Spring 1973), 87-
     90.

760 Raban, Jonathan. "Exactitudes." The New Statesman,
     78 (28 November 1969), 783-784.

761 Read, Herbert. "Introduction." Writers on Them-
     selves (London: Cox and Lyman, 1964), iii-iv.

762 Robins, Corinne. "Four Young Poets." Mademoiselle,
     48 (January 1959), 34-35, 85.

763 Roland, Laurin K. "Sylvia Plath's 'Lesbos': A Self
     Divided." Concerning Poetry, 9 (1976), 61-65.

764 Romano, John. "Sylvia Plath Reconsidered." Commen-
     tary, 57 (April 1974), 47-52.

765 Rosenblatt, Jon. "'The Couriers.'" Explicator, 34
     (December 1975), Item 28.

766 Rosenstein, Harriet. "Reconsidering Sylvia Plath."
     Ms., 1 (September 1972), 44-51, 96-99. [Illustra-
     ted.]

767 Rosenthal, M. L. "Other Confessional Poets: Sylvia
     Plath." In Rosenthal's The New Poets: American
     and British Poetry Since World War II (New York:
     Oxford University Press, 1967), 79-89. Reprinted
     with slight revisions as "Sylvia Plath and Confes-
     sional Poetry" in The Art of Sylvia Plath, ed.
     Charles Newman (Bloomington: Indiana University
     Press, 1970; London: Faber & Faber, 1970), 69-
     76.

768 _____. "Poetic Theory of Some Contemporary Poets."
     Salmagundi, 4 (Winter 1966/67), 69-77.

769 _____. "Uncertain Odysseus: The Critic of Current
Poetry." Shenandoah, 19 (May 1968), 59-66.

770 Salamon, Lynda B. "'Double, Double': Perception in
the Poetry of Sylvia Plath." Spirit, 38 (1970),
34-39.

771 Scheerer, Constance. "The Deathly Paradise of Sylvia
Plath." Antioch Review, 34 (Summer 1976), 469-
480.

772 Schrickx, W. "De Dichtkunst van Sylvia Plath."
Dietsche Warande en Belfort, 116 (1971), 191-210.

773 Schwartz, M. M., and C. Bollas. "The Absence at
the Center: Sylvia Plath and Suicide." Criticism,
18 (Spring 1976), 147-172.

774 Sergeant, Howard. "Poetry Review." English, 14
(Summer 1962), 73-75.

775 Sexton, Anne. "The Barfly Ought to Sing." Tri-Quarterly, 7 (Fall 1966), 89-94. Reprinted in The Art
of Sylvia Plath, ed. Charles Newman (Bloomington:
Indiana University Press, 1970; London: Faber &
Faber, 1970), 174-181.

776 Shook, Margaret. "Sylvia Plath: The Poet and the
College." Smith Alumnae Quarterly, 63 (April
1972), 4-9.

777 Sigmund, Elizabeth. "To the Editor: The Bell Jar."
Times Literary Supplement, 30 November 1973,
1477.

778 Smith, Pamela. "Architectonics: Sylvia Plath's Colossus." Ariel: A Review of International English
Literature, 4 (January 1973), 4-21.

779 _____. "The Unitive Urge in the Poetry of Sylvia
Plath." New England Quarterly, 45 (September
1972), 323-339.

780 Smith, Stan. "Attitudes Counterfeiting Life: The Irony
of Artifice in Sylvia Plath's The Bell Jar." Critical Quarterly, 17 (Autumn 1975), 247-260.

781 Sobski, Jozefa. "Sylvia Plath." Mejane, 2 (July 1973), 13.

782 Spendal, R. J. "Sylvia Plath's 'Cut.'" Modern Poetry Studies, 6 (Autumn 1975), 128-134.

783 Spender, Stephen. "Warnings from the Grave." New Republic, 154 (18 June 1966), 23, 25-26. Reprinted in The Art of Sylvia Plath, ed. Charles Newman (Bloomington: Indiana University Press, 1970; London: Faber & Faber, 1970), 199-203.

784 Stade, George. "Introduction." In Nancy Steiner's A Closer Look at Ariel: A Memory of Sylvia Plath (New York: Harper Magazine Press, 1973; New York: Popular Library Paperback, 1974; London: Faber & Faber, 1974; London: Faber & Faber, 1974 [paperback]), 3-30.

785 Stainton, Rita T. "Vision and Voice in Three Poems by Sylvia Plath." Windless Orchard, 17 (Spring 1974), 31-36.

786 Starbuck, G. "Spectator's Notebook." The Spectator, 210 (22 February 1963), 220.

787 "The State of Poetry--A Symposium." The Review, 29-30 (Spring/Summer 1972), 3-73.

788 Steiner, George. "'Dying Is an Art.'" The Reporter, 33 (7 October 1965), 51-54. Reprinted in part as "'Dying Is an Art': The Poetry of Sylvia Plath, '55" in Smith Alumnae Quarterly, 57 (Winter 1966), 85-87. Reprinted complete in George Steiner's Language and Silence (London: Faber & Faber, 1967, 324-331; New York: Atheneum, 1967, 295-302). Reprinted in The Art of Sylvia Plath, ed. Charles Newman (Bloomington: Indiana University Press, 1970; London: Faber & Faber, 1970), 211-218.

789 _____. "In Extremis." Cambridge Review, 90 (7 February 1969), 247-249. Reprinted in The Cambridge Mind, ed. Eric Homberger et al. (Boston: Little, Brown, 1970), 303-307.

790 Steiner, Nancy Hunter. "Sylvia Plath: A Roommate's

Memoir. " Mademoiselle, 76 (January 1973), 96-
100. Excerpted from Nancy Steiner's A Closer
Look at Ariel: A Memory of Sylvia Plath (New
York: Harper Magazine Press, 1973; New York:
Popular Library Paperback, 1974; London: Faber
& Faber, 1974; London: Faber & Faber, 1974
[paperback]).

791 Stilwell, Robert L. "The Multiplying Entities: D. H.
Lawrence and Five Other Poets. " Sewanee Review,
76 (July-September 1968), 520-535.

792 Stoianoff, Ellen A. "Sylvia Plath: Three Poems and a
Remembrance. " Mademoiselle, 73 (September
1971), 160-161.

793 "The Story of an American Poet's Love Affair with
Europe. " The Sunday Times [London], 18 April
1976, 33-34. [Illustrated.]

794 Sumner, Nan McCowan. "Sylvia Plath. " Research
Studies (Washington State University), 38 (June
1970), 112-121.

795 "Sylvia Plath. " In Contemporary Authors: A Bio-bib-
liographical Guide to Current Authors and Their
Works, ed. James E. Ethridge, Barbara Kopala,
and Carolyn Riley, Vols. 19-20 (Detroit: Gale
Research Company, 1968), 342-344.

796 "Sylvia Plath Memoir Dropped. " The Times [London],
19 November 1971, 14d.

797 "Sylvia Plath, 1932-1963. " In 200 Contemporary Authors, ed. Barbara Harte and Carolyn Riley (Detroit: Gale Research Company, 1969), 214-216.

798 Talbot, Norman. "Sisterhood Is Powerful: The Moon
in Sylvia Plath's Poetry. " New Poetry (Sydney),
21 (June 1973), 23-36.

799 Tanner, Tony. "Interior Spaciousness--Car, Bell Jar,
Tunnel and Bone. " In Tanner's City of Words:
American Fiction 1950-1970 (London: Jonathan
Cape, 1971; New York: Harper & Row, 1971).

800 Taylor, Andrew. "Sylvia Plath's Mirror and Beehive. "
Meanjin, 33 (September 1974), 256-265.

801 Thwaite, Anthony. "'I have never been so happy in my
     life': On Sylvia Plath. " Encounter, 46 (June 1976),
     64-67.

802 Uroff, Margaret D. "Sylvia Plath on Motherhood. "
     Midwest Quarterly, 15 (October 1973), 70-90.

803 _____. "Sylvia Plath's 'Tulips.'" Paunch, 42-43:
     90-96.

804 _____. "Sylvia Plath's Women. " Concerning Poetry,
     7, no. 1, 45-56.

805 Vendler, Helen. "La Poesia de Sylvia Plath. " Plural,
     33 (1974), 6-14.

806 Weinraub, Bernard. "Literary Dispute Arises over
     Sylvia Plath's Death. " New York Times, 23 No-
     vember 1971, 54.

807 Winter, Helmut. "Sylvia Plath. " In Amerikanische
     Literatur der Gegenwart, ed. Martin Christadler
     (Stuttgart: Alfred Kröner, 1973), 634-651.

808 Yoshida, Sachiko. "Incense of Death: Sylvia Plath no
     Sonzai no Kaku. " Eigo Seinen, 120: 488-489.
     [In Japanese.]

809 Zollman, Sol. "Sylvia Plath and Imperialist Culture. "
     Literature and Ideology, 1 (1969), 11-22.

C. REVIEWS

** ARIEL **

810 "Along the Edge." Times Literary Supplement, 25 November 1965, 1071.

811 Alvarez, A. "Poetry in Extremis." The Observer,
14 March 1965, 26.

812 "Ariel." Publishers Weekly, 194 (26 August 1968), 273.

813 Baro, Gene. "Varied Quintet." New York Times Book
Review, 26 June 1966, 10, 12, 14.

814 Bewley, Marius. "Poetry Chronicle." Hudson Review,
19 (Autumn 1966), 479-493.

815 "The Blood Jet Is Poetry." Time, 87 (10 June 1966),
118-120. [Illustrated.]

816 Booklist, 63 (15 February 1967), 613.

817 Brinnin, John Malcolm. "Plath, Jarrell, Kinnell,
Smith." Partisan Review, 34 (Winter 1967), 156-
160.

818 Burke, Herbert C. Library Journal, 91 (1 June 1966),
2851.

819 Choice, 3 (October 1966), 650.

820 Dale, Peter. "O Honey Bees Come Build." Agenda,
4 (Summer 1966), 49-55.

821 Davis, Douglas M. "In the Flow of Poetry, the Ladies
Flourish." National Observer, 6 (6 February 1967),
31.

822   Davison, Peter. "Inhabited by a Cry: The Last
      Poetry of Sylvia Plath. " Atlantic, 218 (August
      1966), 76-77.

823   Drake, Barbara. "Perfection Is Terrible; It Cannot
      Have Children. " Northwest Review, 9 (Summer
      1967), 101-103.

824   Feldman, Irving. "The Religion of One. " Book Week,
      19 June 1966, 3.

825   Friedberg, Martha. "With Feeling and Color. " Chi-
      cago Sunday Tribune Books Today, 26 June 1966, 6.

826   Furbank, P. N. "New Poetry. " The Listener, 73
      (11 March 1965), 379.

827   Hope, Francis. "Suffer and Observe. " The New States-
      man, 69 (30 April 1965), 687-688.

828   Horder, John. "Ariel. " Outposts, 66 (Autumn 1965),
      24-25.

829   Howes, Barbara. "A Note on Ariel. " Massachusetts
      Review, 8 (Winter 1967), 225-226.

830   Jaffe, Dan. "An All-American Muse. " Saturday Re-
      view, 49 (15 October 1966), 29-31.

831   Johnson, B. S. "Measure, Chaos and Indifference. "
      Ambit, no. 24 (1965), 45-46.

832   Kell, Richard. "The Foil of Despair. " Manchester
      Guardian, 18 March 1965, 11.

833   Kenner, Hugh. "On Ariel. " Triumph, September 1966,
      33-34.

834   Kirkus Reviews, 34 (15 March 1966), 351.

835   Lask, Thomas. "A Kind of Heroism. " New York
      Times, 8 June 1966, 45.

836   Maddocks, Melvin. "Sylvia Plath: The Cult and the
      Poems. " Christian Science Monitor, 30 June 1966,
      13.

837 Morse, Samuel French. "Poetry 1966." Contemporary
     Literature, 9 (Winter 1968), 112-129.

838 "Notes on Current Books." Virginia Quarterly Review,
     42 (Autumn 1966), cxl.

839 Parker, Derek. "Ariel, Indeed." Poetry Review, 56
     (Summer 1965), 118-120.

840 "Poems for the Good-Hearted." The Times [London],
     4 November 1965, 15b.

841 Press, John. "Two Poets." Punch, 248 (31 March
     1965), 486.

842 "Reference Books." New York Quarterly, 12 (Autumn
     1972), 110-111.

843 Rosenthal, M. L. "Poets of the Dangerous Way."
     The Spectator, 214 (19 March 1965), 367.

844 Ross, Alan. "Selected Books." London Magazine,
     New Series 5 (May 1965), 99-101.

845 "Russian Roulette." Newsweek, 67 (20 June 1966), 110.

846 Sealy, D. Dublin Magazine, Summer 1966, 92.

847 Sergeant, Howard. "Poetry Review." English, 16
     (Spring 1966), 30-32.

848 Skelton, Robin. "Britannia's Muse Revisited." Massa-
     chusetts Review, 6 (Autumn 1965), 829-839.

849 Smith, William Jay. "New Books of Poems." Har-
     per's, 233 (August 1966), 92.

850 Stephens, Alan. "Twelve New Books of Poetry, 1966."
     Denver Quarterly, 1 (Winter 1967), 101-112.

851 Taylor, Elinor Ross. "Sylvia Plath's Last Poems."
     Poetry, 109 (January 1967), 260-262.

852 Tillinghast, Richard. "Worlds of Their Own." Southern
     Review, 5 (Spring 1969), 582-596.

** THE BED BOOK **

853 Croome, Lesley. "Pictures of the Mind." Times
    Literary Supplement, 2 April 1976, 396.

** THE BELL JAR **

854 Adams, Phoebe. "Short Reviews: Books." Atlantic,
    227 (May 1971), 114.

855 "The Bell Jar." Publishers Weekly, 199 (1 March
    1971), 54.

856 "The Bell Jar." Publishers Weekly, 201 (28 February
    1972), 74.

857 "Best Books for Young Adults." Booklist, 68 (1 April
    1972), 664.

858 "Best Books for Young Adults 1971." Top of the News,
    28 (April 1972), 313.

859 Best Sellers, 32 (1 May 1971), 71.

860 "Book World Picks Fifty Notable Books of 1971."
    Washington Post Book World, 5 December 1971, 5.

861 "Books for Young Adults." Library Journal, 97 (15
    May 1972), 1887.

862 Butler, Rupert. "New American Fiction: Three Dis-
    appointing Novels--But One Good One." Time and
    Tide, 44 (31 January 1963), 34.

863 Cox, C. B. "Editorial." Critical Quarterly, 8 (Autumn
    1966), 195.

864 Davenport, Guy. "Novels in Braille." National Review,
    23 (18 May 1971), 538.

865 Duffy, Martha. "Lady Lazarus." Time, 97 (21 June
    1971), K7-K9.

866 Harris, M. West Coast Review, 7 (October 1973), 54.

867 Hill, William B. "Fiction." America, 125 (20 Novem-
    ber 1971), 432.

868 Hurlbert, Joyce. "Book Reviews." West Coast Review
     7, (January 1973), 82.

869 Kirkus Reviews, 39 (1 February 1971), 135-136.

870 Lehmann-Haupt, Christopher. "An American Edition--
     at Last." New York Times, 16 April 1971, 35.

871 Lerner, Lawrence. "New Novels." "The Listener, 69
     (31 January 1963), 215.

872 Lilenthal, Mark. San Francisco Chronicle, This World
     Magazine, 10 March 1963, 33.

873 Maddocks, Melvin. "A Vacuum Abhorred." Christian
     Science Monitor, 15 April 1971, 11.

874 Maloff, Saul. "Waiting for the Voice to Crack." New
     Republic, 164 (8 May 1971), 33-35.

875 Morse, J. Mitchell. "Fiction Chronicle." Hudson Re-
     view, 24 (Autumn 1971), 526-544.

876 Moss, Howard. "Dying: An Introduction." The New
     Yorker, 47 (10 July 1971), 73-75.

877 Murray, Michele. "Prose and Cons." National Ob-
     server, 10 (31 May 1971), 18.

878 Nilsen, Aleen Pace. "Books for Young Adults: Death
     and Dying--Facts, Fiction, Folklore." English
     Journal, 62 (November 1973), 1188.

879 "Notable Nominations." American Libraries, 2 (July
     1971), 762.

880 "Notes on Current Books." Virginia Quarterly Review,
     47 (Summer 1971), xcvi.

881 O'Hara, J. D. "An American Dream Girl." Washing-
     ton Post Book World, 11 April 1971, 3.

882 O'Hara, T. Best Sellers, 31 (1 June 1971), 123.

883 Paterno, Domenica. "Poetry." Library Journal, 96
     (1 October 1971), 3141.

884 Petersen, Clarence. "Paperbacks." Washington Post Book World, 30 April 1972, 8.

885 Pettingell, Phoebe. "The Art of Dying." New Leader, 54 (28 June 1971), 19-20.

886 Raven, Simon. "The Trouble with Phaedra." The Spectator, 210 (15 February 1963), 202-203.

887 Reed, Coats. Library Journal, 97 (15 February 1972), 791-792.

888 Rosenthal, Lucy. "The Bell Jar." Saturday Review, 54 (24 April 1971), 42.

889 Rosenthal, M. L. "Blood and Plunder." The Spectator, 217 (30 September 1966), 418.

890 Scholes, Robert. "The Bell Jar." New York Times Book Review, 11 April 1971, 7.

891 "A Selection of Recent Titles: Fiction." New York Times Book Review, 6 June 1971, 3. Reprinted in the New York Times Book Review, 5 December 1971, 78-82.

892 Spacks, Patricia Meyer. "A Chronicle of Women." Hudson Review, 25 (Spring 1972), 157-170.

893 Taubman, Robert. "Anti-heroes." The New Statesman, 65 (25 January 1963), 127-128.

894 "Uncles' War." The New Statesman, 72 (16 September 1966), 401-402.

895 "Under the Skin." Times Literary Supplement, 25 January 1963, 53.

896 Wall, Stephen. The Observer, 11 September 1966, 27.

897 Wolff, Geoffrey. "The Bell Jar." Newsweek, 77 (19 April 1971), 120.

** THE COLOSSUS **

898 Alvarez, A. "The Poet and the Poetess." The Ob-

server, 18 December 1960, 12.

899 Bergonzi, Bernard. "The Ransom Note. " Manchester
      Guardian, 25 November 1960, 9.

900 Blackburn, Thomas. "Poetic Knowledge. " The New
      Statesman, 60 (24 December 1960), 1016.

901 Booklist, 59 (1 November 1962), 200.

902 Burke, Herbert C. "Poetry. " Library Journal, 87
      (15 June 1962), 2385-2386.

903 "Chained to the Parish Pump. " Times Literary Sup-
      plement, 16 March 1967, 220.

904 Davis, Douglas M. "More on the Poetry Shelves. "
      National Observer, 8 (17 March 1969), 21.

905 Dearmer, Geoffrey. "Sows' Ears and Silk Purses. "
      Poetry Review, 52 (July-September 1961), 166-168.

906 Dickcy, William. "Responsibilities. " Kenyon Review,
      24 (Autumn 1962), 756-764.

907 Dickinson, Peter. "Some Poets. " Punch, 239 (7 De-
      cember 1960), 829.

908 Dyson, A. E. "Reviews and Comments. " Critical
      Quarterly, 3 (Summer 1961), 181-185.

909 Fuller, Roy. "Book Reviews. " London Magazine, 8
      (March 1961), 69-70.

910 Hamilton, Ian. "Poetry. " London Magazine, New
      Series 3 (July 1963), 54-57.

911 Hayman, Ronald. "Personal Poetry. " Encounter, 29
      (December 1967), 86-87.

912 Howard, Richard. "Five Poets. " Poetry, 101 (March
      1963), 412-418. Reprinted in Poetry, 121 (Octo-
      ber 1972), 54-59.

913 Hurd, Pearl Strachan. "In Larger Rhythm. " Christian
      Science Monitor, 20 August 1962, 11.

914 "Innocence and Experience." Times Literary Supplement, 18 August 1961, 550.

915 Jerome, Judson. "A Poetry Chronicle--Part I." Antioch Review, 23 (Spring 1963), 110-111.

916 King, Nicholas. "Poetry: A Late Summer Roundup." New York Herald-Tribune Book Review, 26 August 1962, 4.

917 Moraes, Dom. "Poems from Many Parts." Time and Tide, 41 (19 November 1960), 143.

918 Myers, E. Lucas. "The Tranquillized Fifties." Sewanee Review, 70 (January-March 1962), 212-220.

919 The Observer, 26 March 1967, 23.

920 Owen, Guy. Books Abroad, 37 (Spring 1963), 209.

921 Press, John. "Four Poets." Punch, 252 (5 April 1967), 508.

922 Rosenthal, M. L. "Metamorphosis of a Book." The Spectator, 218 (21 April 1967), 456-57.

923 Sergeant, Howard. "Poetry Review." English, 13 (Spring 1961), 156-158.

924 Simon, John. "More Brass than Enduring." Hudson Review, 15 (Autumn 1962), 455-468.

925 Stubblefield, Charles. "A Craft." Prairie Schooner, 45 (Spring 1971), 83.

926 Symons, Julian. "The Old Enemies." The New Statesman, 73 (7 April 1967), 479.

927 Tulip, James. "Three Women Poets." Poetry Australia, 19 (December 1967), 35-40.

928 Wain, John. "Farewell to the World." The Spectator, 206 (13 January 1961), 50.

929 Whittemore, Reed. "The Colossus and Other Poems." Carleton Miscellany, 3 (Fall 1962), 89.

** CROSSING THE WATER **

930   Aird, Eileen. "Reviews and Comment." Critical Quar-
      terly, 12 (Autumn 1971), 286-288.

931   Booklist, 68 (15 November 1971), 266.

932   Boyers, Robert. "On Sylvia Plath." Salmagundi, 21
      (Winter 1973), 96-104.

933   Davison, Peter. "Three Visionary Poets." Atlantic,
      229 (February 1972), 105-106.

934   Eagleton, Terry. "New Poetry." Stand, 13 (1971-72),
      76.

935   Fuller, John. The Listener, 85 (3 June 1971), 728-
      729.

936   Howes, Victor. "I Am Silver and Exact." Christian
      Science Monitor, 30 September 1971, 8.

937   Jacobson, Dan. "Mirrors Can Kill: The Artistic Mar-
      tyrdom of Sylvia Plath." The Listener, 86 (7 Oc-
      tober 1971), 482.

938   Kameen, Paul. Best Sellers, 31 (1 November 1071),
      347-348.

939   Kirkus Reviews, 39 (1 July 1971), 727.

940   Kramer, Victor. "Life-and-Death Dialectics." Modern
      Poetry Studies, 3 (1972), 40-42.

941   Melander, Ingrid. Moderna Språk, 65 (1971), 360-363.

942   "1971: A Selection of Noteworthy Titles: Poetry."
      New York Times Book Review, 5 December 1971,
      86.

943   "Notes on Current Books." Virginia Quarterly Review,
      48 (Winter 1972), xxii.

944   The Observer, 3 October 1971, 36.

945   Paterno, Domenica. "Poetry." Library Journal, 96
      (1 October 1971), 3141.

946 Pritchard, William H.   "Youngsters, Middlesters, and
     Some Old Boys. " Hudson Review, 25 (Spring 1972),
     119-134.

947 "Reservations. " Antioch Review, 31 (Winter 1971/72),
     587.

948 Richmond, Lee J.   "Books Covered and Uncovered. "
     Erasmus Review, 1 (1971), 160-162.

949 Scruton, Roger.   "Sylvia Plath and the Savage God. "
     The Spectator, 227 (18 December 1971), 890.

950 Sergeant, Howard.   "Poetry Review. " English, 20
     (Autumn 1971), 106-109.

951 Skelton, Robin.   "Poetry. " Malahat Review, 20 (Octo-
     ber 1971), 137-138.

952 Vendler, Helen.   "Crossing the Water. " New York
     Times Book Review, 10 October 1971, 4, 48.

953 West, Paul.   "'Fido Littlesoul, the Bowel's Familiar.'"
     Washington Post Book World, 9 January 1972, 8.

954 "A World in Disintegration. " Times Literary Supple-
     ment, 24 December 1971, 1602.

**   LETTERS HOME   **

955 Ackroyd, Peter.   "Dear Mummy, I Hate You. " The
     Spectator, 236 (24 April 1976), 21.

956 Adams, Phoebe-Lou.   "PLA. " Atlantic, 237 (February
     1976), 111.

957 Booklist, 72 (15 October 1975), 272-273.

958 Byatt, A. S.   "Mirror, Mirror on the Wall. " The New
     Statesman, 91 (23 April 1976), 541-542.

959 Choice, 13 (May 1976), 371.

960 Cosgrave, Mary Silva.   "Outlook Tower. " Horn Book,
     52 (April 1976), 185.

961 Crain, Jane Larkin. "Letters Home: Correspondence
     1950-1963. " Saturday Review, New Series 3 (15
     November 1975), 26.

962 Dinnage, Rosemary. "A Girl from Wellesley. " Times
     Literary Supplement, 23 April 1976, 480.

963 Duffy, Martha. "Two Lives. " Time, 106 (24 November
     1975), 101-102.

964 The Economist, 259 (1 May 1976), 124.

965 Eriksson, Pamela Dale. "Sylvia Plath: Letters Home:
     Correspondence 1950-1963. " Unisa English Studies,
     14 (September 1976), 95-97.

966 Ferrier, Carole. "Sylvia Plath's Intercepted Letters. "
     Nation Review (Australia), 6-12 August 1976, 1056.

967 Howard, Maureen. "Letters Home. " New York Times
     Book Review, 14 December 1975, 1-2.

968 Jefferson, Margo. "Who Was Sylvia?" Newsweek, 86
     (22 December 1975), 83.

969 Kenner, Hugh. National Review, 18 (30 April 1976),
     459-460.

970 Kirkus Reviews, 43 (15 September 1975), 1103.

971 Lehmann-Haupt, Christopher. "From Outside the Bell
     Jar. " New York Times, 9 December 1975, 39.

972 "Letters Home. " Publishers Weekly, 208 (18 August
     1975), 58.

973 "Letters Home: Correspondence 1950-1963. " The New
     Yorker, 51 (22 December 1975), 95-96.

974 Maloff, Saul. Commonweal, 103 (4 June 1976), 371-
     374.

975 The Observer, 18 April 1976, 23.

976 Reed, Nancy Gail. "Still Those Ellipses.... " Christian
     Science Monitor, 7 January 1976, 23.

977 Rosenstein, Harriet. "To the Most Wonderful Mummy
     ... A Girl Ever Had. " Ms. , 4 (December 1975), 45-
     49.

978 Rubenstein, Roberta. "Virginia Woolf and Sylvia Plath:
     Inner Truths. " Progressive, 40 (March 1976),
     41-42.

979 Tyler, Anne. "'The Voice Hangs On, Gay, Tremulous.'"
     National Observer, 15 (10 January 1976), 19.

980 Zaidman, Laura. "Biography. " Library Journal, 100
     (15 October 1975), 1916.

** WINTER TREES **

981 Baumgaertner, Jill. "Four Poets: Blood Type New. "
     Cresset, 36 (April 1973), 16-19.

982 Booklist, 69 (1 January 1973), 424.

983 "Books for Young Adults. " Booklist, 69 (15 January
     1973), 490.

984 Brownjohn, Alan. "Awesome Fragments. " The New
     Statesman, 82 (1 October 1971), 446-448.

985 Choice, 9 (February 1973), 1592.

986 Cotter, James Finn. "Women Poets: Malign Neglect?"
     America, 128 (17 February 1973), 140-142.

987 Dunn, Douglas. "King Offa Alive and Dead: Ten
     Poets. " Encounter, 38 (January 1972), 67.

988 Gordon, Jan B. "Saint Sylvia. " Modern Poetry Studies,
     2 (1972), 282-286.

989 Grant, Damian. "Reviews and Comment. " Critical
     Quarterly, 14 (Spring 1972), 92-95.

990 Howes, Victor. "Sometimes, a Walker of Air. "
     Christian Science Monitor, 4 October 1972, 11.

991 Hughes, Ted. "Winter Trees. " Poetry Book Society
     Bulletin, 70 (Autumn 1971).

992 Kameen, Paul. Best Sellers, 32 (15 January 1973),
     474-475.

993 Kirkus Reviews, 40 (15 July 1972), 846. Reprinted in
     Kirkus Reviews, 40 (15 August 1972), 956.

994 Kramer, Victor A. "Life-and-Death Dialectics."
     Modern Poetry Studies, 3 (1972), 40-42.

995 Library Journal, 97 (1 May 1972), 1744.

996 Melander, Ingrid. Moderna Språk, 65 (1971), 360-363.

997 "1972: A Selection of Noteworthy Titles: Poetry."
     New York Times Book Review, 3 December 1972,
     84.

998 Nye, Robert. "A Bright Pane Broken." The Times
     [London], 30 September 1971, 12a.

999 Oates, Joyce Carol. "An Eerie Fusion of Power and
     Helplessness." Library Journal, 97 (1 November
     1972), 3595.

1000 _____. "Winter Trees." New York Times Book
     Review, 19 November 1972, 7, 14.

1001 Pevear, Richard. "Poetry Chronicle." Hudson Re-
     view, 26 (Spring 1973), 192-218.

1002 Porter, Peter. "Collecting Her Strength." The New
     Statesman, 81 (4 June 1971), 774-775.

1003 "Random Notes." National Review, 24 (9 June 1972),
     650.

1004 Schott, Webster. "The Cult of Plath." The Washing-
     ton Post Book World, 1 October 1972, 3.

1005 Scruton, Roger. "Sylvia Plath and The Savage God."
     The Spectator, 227 (18 December 1971), 890.

1006 Sergeant, Howard. "Poetry Review." English, 21
     (Summer 1972), 75.

1007 Smith, Raymond. "Late Harvest." Modern Poetry
     Studies, 3 (1972), 91-93.

1008   Storey, Elizabeth. "Non-Fiction." Library Journal,
       98 (15 January 1972), 276.

1009   "A World in Disintegration." Times Literary Supple-
       ment, 24 December 1971, 1602.

D. DISSERTATIONS/MONOGRAPHS

1010 Aird, Eileen M. "Sylvia Plath: An Introduction to Her Life and Art." M. Litt., Newcastle upon Tyne, 1968. Also see Aird's later book, Sylvia Plath: Her Life and Work (item 603).

1011 Balitas, Vincent Daniel. "Sylvia Plath, Poet." Ph. D., Indiana University of Pennsylvania, 1973.

1012 Barnard, Caroline King. "God's Lioness: The Poetry of Sylvia Plath." Ph. D., Brown University, 1973.

1013 Broe, Mary Lynn. "Persona and Poetic: The Poetry of Sylvia Plath." Ph. D., University of Connecticut, 1975.

1014 Capek, Mary Ellen Stagg. "'Perfection Is Terrible': A Study of Sylvia Plath's Poetry." Ph. D., University of Wisconsin, 1973.

1015 Cloud, Jeraldine Neifer. "Robert Lowell, Sylvia Plath, and the Confessional Mode in Contemporary Poetry." Ph. D., Emory University, 1976.

1016 Gordon, Lydia Caroline. "'From Stone to Cloud': A Critical Study of Sylvia Plath." Ph. D., University of Pennsylvania, 1975.

1017 Jones, E. H. "The Woman as Hero: A Study of the Poetry and Fiction of Sylvia Plath." Ph. D., Essex, 1971.

1018 Kroll, Judith. "Chapters in a Mythology: The Poetic Vision of Sylvia Plath." Ph. D., Yale University, 1974. Also see Kroll's later book, Chapters in a Mythology: The Poetry of Sylvia Plath (item 606).

101

1019 Levine, Ellen Sue. "From Water to Land: The Poetry
      of Sylvia Plath, James Wright, and W. S. Mer-
      win. " Ph. D. , University of Washington, 1974.

1020 McClave, Heather. "Situations of the Mind: Studies
      of Center and Periphery in Dickinson, Stevens,
      Ammons, and Plath. " Ph. D. , Yale University,
      1975.

1021 Megna, Jerome Francis. "The Two-World Division in
      the Poetry of Sylvia Plath. " Ed. D. , Ball State
      University, 1972.

1022 Pisapia, Biancamaria. "L'arte di Sylvia Plath. "
      Roma: Bulzoni, 1972. (Istituto di Letteratura
      Inglese e Americana Studi e Ricerche.)

1023 Ries, Lawrence Robert. "The Response to Violence
      in Contemporary British Poetry. " Ph. D. , South-
      ern Illinois University, 1971.

1024 Rosenblatt, Jon Michael. "The Poetic Development of
      Sylvia Plath: A Study in Theme and Image. "
      Ph. D. , University of North Carolina at Chapel
      Hill, 1975.

1025 Rosenstein, Harriet Cecile. "Sylvia Plath: 1932-
      1952. " Ph. D. , Brandeis University, 1973.

1026 Snively, Susan Rumble. "The Language of Necessity:
      The Poetry of Sylvia Plath. " Ph. D. , Boston Uni-
      versity, 1976.

1027 Stainton, Rita Tomasallo. "The Magician's Girl:
      Power and Vulnerability in the Poetry of Sylvia
      Plath. " Ph. D. , Rutgers University, 1975.

1028 Stone, Carole Barbara. "Sylvia Plath's Spiritual
      Quest. " Ph. D. , Fordham University, 1976.

1029 Wallenstein, Barry. "Monarch Literature Notes on
      Plath's The Bell Jar. " New York: Monarch
      Press, 1975.

1030 Wegs, Joyce Markert. "The Grotesque in Some Ameri-
      can Novels of the Nineteen-Sixties: Ken Kesey,
      Joyce Carol Oates, Sylvia Plath. " Ph. D. , Univer-
      sity of Illinois at Urbana-Champaign, 1973.

E. POEMS

1031 Berryman, John. "I'm cross with god who has wrecked this generation" (Dream Song 153) and "Them lady poets must not marry, pal" (Dream Song 187). In Berryman's His Toy, His Dream, His Rest (New York: Farrar, Straus & Giroux, 1968), 82, 116. Reprinted in Berryman's The Dream Songs (New York: Farrar, Straus & Giroux, 1969), 172, 206.

1032 Garitano, Rita. "A Room of Her Own." In Garitano's We Do What We Can (Tucson: Desert First Works, 1975). Reprinted in The Face of Poetry, ed. LaVerne Harrell Clark and Mary MacArthur (Arlington, Virginia: Gallimaufry, 1976), 85.

1033 Morgan, Robin. "Arraignment 1." In Morgan's Monster (New York: Random House, 1972), 76-78.

1034 Rukeyser, Muriel. "Not To Be Printed, Not To Be Said, Not To Be Thought." In Rukeyser's The Gates (New York: McGraw-Hill, 1976), 63.

1035 Sexton, Anne. "Sylvia's Death." In Sexton's Live or Die (New York: Oxford University Press, 1967), 38-40. Reprinted in The Art of Sylvia Plath, ed. Charles Newman (Bloomington: Indiana University Press, 1970; London: Faber & Faber, 1970), 179-181.

1036 Talbot, Norman. "For Sylvia Plath: February 1963." In Poetry Australia, 48 (1973), 13-16.

1037 Wakoski, Diane. "The Water Element Song for Sylvia." In Wakoski's Greed, Parts 8, 9, 11 (Santa Barbara, California: Black Sparrow Press, 1973), 19-31.

1038   Wilbur, Richard.   "Cottage Street, 1953." In Wilbur's
          The Mind Reader (New York: Harcourt Brace
          Jovanovich, 1976), 19.

F.   BIBLIOGRAPHIES

1039   Cunningham, Stuart.   "Bibliography: Sylvia Plath. "
       Hecate (Australia), 1 (July 1975), 95-112.

1040   Homberger, Eric.   A Chronological Checklist of the
       Periodical Publications of Sylvia Plath.   Exeter,
       England: University of Exeter, 1970 (American
       Arts Pamphlet No. 1).

1041   Kinzie, Mary.   "An Informal Check List of Criticism. "
       In The Art of Sylvia Plath, ed.   Charles Newman
       (Bloomington: Indiana University Press, 1970;
       London: Faber & Faber, 1970), 283-304.

1042   _____, Daniel Lynn Conrad and Suzanne D.
       Kurman.   "Bibliography. "   In The Art of Sylvia
       Plath, ed.   Charles Newman (Bloomington: Indiana
       University Press, 1970; London: Faber & Faber,
       1070), 305-319.

1043   Walsh, Thomas P. , and Cameron Northouse.   Sylvia
       Plath and Anne Sexton: A Reference Guide.
       Boston: G. K. Hall, 1974.

III

APPENDICES

A. CHRONOLOGY OF PLATH'S PUBLICATIONS
(asterisk indicates a prose work)

1950

*"Youth's Plea for World Peace," with Perry Norton.
Christian Science Monitor, 16 March 1950, 19.

*"And Summer Will Not Come Again." Seventeen, 9 (August
1950), 191, 275-276.

"Bitter Strawberries." Christian Science Monitor, 11 August
1950, 17.

1951

*"As a Baby-Sitter Sees It." Christian Science Monitor, 6
November 1951, 19, and 7 November 1951, 21.

1952

*"Sunday at the Mintons." Mademoiselle, 35 (August 1952),
255, 371-378.

*"The Perfect Setup." Seventeen, 11 (August 1952), 76,
100-104.

"White Phlox." Christian Science Monitor, 27 August, 1952,
12.

*"Sunday at the Mintons." Smith Review, Fall 1952, 3-9.

"Twelfth Night." Seventeen, 11 (December 1952).

1953

*"Initiation. "   Seventeen, 12 (January 1953), 65, 92-94.

[Three Poems.]   Smith Review, Spring 1953, 13, 22.
   "Mad Girl's Love Song"
   "To Eva Descending the Stair"
   "Doomsday"

"The Suitcases Are Packed Again. "   Seventeen, 12 (March
   1953).

[Three Works.]   Mademoiselle, 37 (August 1953), 235, 290-
   291, 358.
   *"Mademoiselle's Last Word on College '53"
   *"Poets on Campus" [interviews with Anthony
      Hecht, Alastair Reid, Richard Wilbur, George
      Steiner, and William Burford]
   "Mad Girl's Love Song"

*"Smith Review Revived. "   Smith Alumnae Quarterly, 45
   (Fall 1953), 26.

1954

[Two Poems.]   Smith Review, Spring 1954, 3, 23.
   "Admonition"
   "Denouement"

"Doomsday. "   Harper's, 208 (May 1954), 29.

"To Eva Descending the Stair. "   Harper's, 209 (September
   1954), 63.

"Go Get the Goodly Squab. "   Harper's, 209 (November 1954),
   47.

[Two Works.]   Smith Review, Fall 1954, 2-5, 18.
   *"In the Mountains"
   "Circus in Three Rings"

1955

Three Works.]   Smith Review, Spring 1955, 12-13, 19-21.
   "Dialogue en Route"

"Danse Macabre"
*"Superman and Paula Brown's New Snowsuit"

"Circus in Three Rings." Atlantic, 196 (August 1955), 68.

"Two Lovers and a Beachcomber by the Real Sea." Mademoiselle, 41 (August 1955), 52, 62.

"Temper of Time." The Nation, 181 (6 August 1955), 119.

"Lament." New Orleans Poetry Journal, 1 (October 1955), 19.

1956

*"Leaves from a Cambridge Notebook." Christian Science Monitor, 5 March 1956, 17, and 6 March 1956, 15.

"B. and K. at the Claridge." Smith Alumnae Quarterly, 48 (Fall 1956), 16-17.

*"The Day Mr. Prescott Died." Granta, 60 (20 October 1956), 20-23.

"Sketchbook of a Spanish Summer." Christian Science Monitor, 5 November 1956, 13; and 6 November 1956, 15. [With four drawings by Sylvia Plath.]

"Ella Mason and Her Eleven Cats." Granta, 60 (10 November 1956), 25.

Two Poems.] The Lyric, 36 (Winter 1956), 10, 11.
"Apotheosis"
"Second Winter"

Two Poems.] Chequer, No. 11 (Winter 1956-57), 4, 6.
"On the Difficulty of Conjuring Up a Dryad"
"Miss Drake Proceeds to Supper"

1957

Six Poems.] Poetry, 89 (January 1957), 231-237.
"Wreath for a Bridal"
"Dream with Clam-Diggers"

"Strumpet Song"
"Two Sisters of Persephone"
"Epitaph for Fire and Flower"
"Metamorphosis"

"Pursuit. " Atlantic, 199 (January 1957), 65.

*"The Wishing Box. " Granta, 61 (26 January 1957), 3-5.

[Three Poems.] Granta, 61 (9 March 1957), 5.
   "Dream with Clam-Diggers"
   "Resolve"
   "Two Lovers and a Beachcomber by the Real Sea"

"Vanity Fair. " Gemini, 1 (Spring 1957).

[Two Poems.] Granta, 61 (4 May 1957), 19.
   "Mad Girl's Love Song"
   "Soliloquy of the Solipsist"

"Black Rook in Rainy Weather. " Granta, 61 (18 May 1957),
   9.

"On the Plethora of Dryads. " New Mexico Quarterly, 27
   (Spring-Summer 1957), 211-212.

"Black Rook in Rainy Weather. " Antioch Review, 17 (June
   1957), 232-233.

[Four Poems.] Poetry, 90 (July 1957), 229-236.
   "The Snowman on the Moor"
   "Sow"
   "Ella Mason and Her Eleven Cats"
   "On the Difficulty of Conjuring Up a Dryad"

*"All the Dead Dears. " Gemini, 1 (Summer 1957), 53-59.

"All the Dead Dears. " Grécourt Review, 1 (November 1957),
   36-37.

[Two Poems.] Accent, 17 (Autumn 1957), 246-48.
   "Recantation"
   "Tinker Jack and the Tidy Wives"

1958

"Two Poems. " London Magazine, 5 (June 1958), 46-48.

"Spinster"
"Black Rook in Rainy Weather"

"Mussel Hunter at Rock Harbor. " New Yorker, 34 (9 August 1958), 22.

*"Beach Plum Season on Cape Cod. " Christian Science Monitor, 14 August 1958, 17.

"Night Walk. " The New Yorker, 34 (11 October 1958), 40.

"Spinster. " Smith Alumnae Quarterly, 49 (Winter 1958), 71.

"Second Winter. " Ladies' Home Journal, 75 (December 1958), 143.

1959

[Two Works.] Mademoiselle, 48 (January 1959), 34-35, 85.
      "The Times Are Tidy"
      *"Four Young Poets" [including Sylvia Plath, in terviewed by Corinne Robins]

"Frog Autumn. " The Nation, 188 (24 January 1959), 74.

"The Companionable Ills. " The Spectator, 202 (30 January 1959), 163.

"Main Street at Midnight. " The Spectator, 202 (13 February 1959), 227.

"Whiteness I Remember. " Christian Science Monitor, 5 March 1959, 12.

"Departure. " The Nation, 188 (7 March 1959), 212.

"Prologue to Spring. " Christian Science Monitor, 23 March 1959, 8.

"Yadwigha, on a Red Couch, Among Lilies (A Sestina for the Douanier). " Christian Science Monitor, 26 March 1959, 8.

"Three Poems. " London Magazine, 6 (March 1959), 33-36.
      "Snakecharmer"
      "The Disquieting Muses"
      "Lorelei"

"The Bull of Bendylaw. " Horn Book, 35 (April 1959), 148.

"Bathtub Battle Scene. " Christian Science Monitor, 25 April
1959, 12.

[Three Poems.] Audience, 6 (Spring 1959), 33-36.
"Full Fathom Five"
"The Hermit at Outermost House"
"Lorelei"

"Sculptor. " Grécourt Review, 2 (May 1959), 282.

"Above the Oxbow. " Christian Science Monitor, 4 May 1959,
8.

"Kitchen of the Fig Tree. " Christian Science Monitor, 5
May 1959, 8.

"A Walk to Withens. " Christian Science Monitor, 6 June
1959, 12.

"Two Poems. " Sewanee Review, 67 (July-September 1959),
446-448.
"Departure of the Ghost"
"Point Shirley"

"Song for a Summer Day. " Christian Science Monitor, 18
August 1959, 8.

"Southern Sunrise. " Christian Science Monitor, 26 August
1959, 8.

[Three Poems.] Poetry, 94 (September 1959), 368-369.
"On the Decline of Oracles"
"The Death of Mythmaking"
"A Lesson in Vengeance"

[Three Poems.] Arts in Society, 1 (Fall 1959), 66-67.
"Aftermath"
"The Goring"
"Sculptor"

"I Want, I Want. " Partisan Review, 26 (Fall 1959), 558.

"Two Poems. " London Magazine, 6 (October 1959), 11-13.
"In Midas' Country"
"The Thin People"

*"Mosaics--An Afternoon of Discovery. " Christian Science
Monitor, 12 October 1959, 15.

*"Explorations Lead to Interesting Discoveries. " Christian
Science Monitor, 19 October 1959, 17.

[Two Poems.] Times Literary Supplement, 6 November
1959, xxiii, xxix.
          "Two Views of a Cadaver Room"
          "The Hermit at Outermost House"

"A Winter's Tale. " The New Yorker, 35 (12 December
1959), 116.

"Dark Wood, Dark Water. " Christian Science Monitor, 17
December 1959, 12.

"Memoirs of a Spinach Picker. " Christian Science Monitor,
29 December 1959, 8.

                       1960

"Two Views of a Cadaver Room. " The Nation, 190 (30 January 1960), 107.

"Man in Black. " The New Yorker, 36 (9 April 1960), 40.

[Two Poems.] Chelsea, 7 (May 1960), 70-71.
          "The Eye-Mote"
          "The Beggars"

"Watercolor of Grantchester Meadows. " The New Yorker,
36 (28 May 1960), 30.

*"The Daughters of Blossom Street. " London Magazine, 7
(May 1960), 34-48.

[Two Poems.] London Magazine, 7 (June 1960), 11-13.
          "The Sleepers"
          "Full Fathom Five"

"Mushrooms. " Harper's, 221 (July 1960), 25.

"A Winter Ship. " Atlantic, 206 (July 1960), 65.

"Poems by Sylvia Plath. " Critical Quarterly, 2 (Summer

1960), 155-157.
    "The Manor Garden"
    "The Beggars"
    "Blue Moles"

"Metaphors for a Pregnant Woman. " Partisan Review, 27
    (Summer 1960), 435.

"The Net Menders. " The New Yorker, 36 (20 August 1960),
    36.

"The Manor Garden. " Atlantic, 206 (September 1960), 52.

[Two Poems.] Kenyon Review, 22 (Autumn 1960), 595-596.
    "The Beekeeper's Daughter"
    "The Colossus"

[Four Poems.] Hudson Review, 13 (Autumn 1960), 413-416.
    "Ouija"
    "Electra on the Azalea Path"
    "Suicide off Egg Rock"
    "Moonrise"

*"The Fifteen-Dollar Eagle. " Sewanee Review, 68 (October-
    December 1960), 603-618.

"Candles. " The Listener, 64 (17 November 1960), 877.

"Medallion. " Critical Quarterly Supplement No. 1, (1960),
    20.

"Flute Notes from a Reedy Pond. " Texas Quarterly, 3
    (Winter 1960), 120.

A Winter Ship. Edinburgh: Tragara Press, 1960. [Limited
    edition.]

The Colossus. London: William Heinemann, 1960.

                          1961

*"The Fifty-Ninth Bear. " London Magazine, 8 (February
    1961), 11-20.

"A Winter Ship. " Encounter, 16 (February 1961), 23.

"Magi. "   The New Statesman, 61 (31 March 1961), 514.

"A Life. "   The Listener, 65 (4 May 1961), 776.

"You're. "   Harper's, 222 (June 1961), 40.

"Two Poems. "   Critical Quarterly, 3 (Summer 1961), 140-141.
        "Private Ground"
        "I Am Vertical"

"On Deck. "   The New Yorker, 37 (22 July 1961), 32.

"Words for a Nursery. "   Atlantic, 208 (August 1961), 66.

"Six Poems. "   London Magazine, New Series 1 (August 1961),
     5-10.
        "Zoo Keeper's Wife"
        "You're"
        "Small Hours"
        "Parliament Hill Fields"
        "Whitsun"
        "Leaving Early"

"Witch Burning. "   Texas Quarterly, 4 (Autumn 1961), 84.

"Mojave Desert. "   The Observer, 19 November 1961, 28.

American Poetry Now: Critical Quarterly Supplement No. 2
        (1961), ed. Sylvia Plath.

                         1962

"The Rival. "   The Observer, 21 January 1962, 31.

"Sleep in the Mojave Desert. "   Harper's, 224 (February
     1962), 36.

[Two Works.] London Magazine, New Series 1 (February
     1962), 15-17, 45-46.
        "In Plaster"
        *'"Context'"

[Five Poems.]   Poetry, 99 (March 1962), 346-351.
        "Stars over the Dordogne"
        "Widow"
        "Face Lift"

"Heavy Women"
"Love Letter"

"Wuthering Heights. " The New Statesman, 63 (16 March
1962), 390.

"The Colossus. " Encounter, 18 (April 1962), 56.

"Tulips. " The New Yorker, 38 (7 April 1962), 40.

*"Pair of Queens. " The New Statesman, 63 (27 April 1962),
602-603. [Review of A Queen of Spain by Peter de
Poinay and Josephine by Hubert Cole.]

*"Oblongs. " The New Statesman, 63 (18 May 1962), 724.
[Review of The Emperor's Oblong Pancakes by Peter
Hughes, The Three Rebels by Tomi Ungerer, The
Funny Thing by Wanda Gag, and Dr. Spock Talks to
Mothers.]

"Private Ground. " Harper's, 225 (August 1962), 55.

"Finisterre. " The Observer, 5 August 1962, 14.

"Blackberrying. " The New Yorker, 38 (15 September 1962),
48.

"The Surgeon at 2 a. m. " The Listener, 68 (20 September
1962), 428.

"Crossing the Water. " The Observer, 23 September 1962,
25.

*"Oregonian Original. " The New Statesman, 63 (9 November
1962), 660. [Review of four children's books.]

"Leaving Early. " Harper's, 225 (December 1962), 82.

"Event. " The Observer, 16 December 1962, 21.

*"Suffering Angel. " The New Statesman, 63 (7 December
1962), 828-829. [Review of Lord Byron's Wife by
Malcolm Elwin.]

"Parliament Hill Fields. " Critical Quarterly Poetry Supplement No. 3 (1962), 10.

The Colossus and Other Poems.   New York: Alfred A.
     Knopf, 1962.

1963

[Two Poems.]   London Magazine, New Series 2 (January
     1963), 14-16.
     "Stopped Dead"
     "The Applicant"

"Winter Trees. "   The Observer, 13 January 1963, 22.

"A Poet's Epitaph" (with a note by A. Alvarez).   The Ob-
     server, 17 February 1963, 23.
          "Edge"
          "The Fearful"
          "Kindness"
          "Contusion"

"A Birthday Present. "   Critical Quarterly, 5 (Spring 1963),
     3-4.

"Seven Poems. "   London Magazine, New Series 3 (April
     1963), 24-32.
          "The Bee Meeting"
          "Stings"
          "Cut"
          "Letter in November"
          "The Couriers"
          "Mary's Song"
          "Years"

"Bees. "   [Two Poems.]   Atlantic, 211 (April 1963), 70-71.
     "The Arrival of the Bee Box"
     "Wintering"

*"America! America!"   Punch, 244 (3 April 1963), 482-484.

"Child. "   The New Statesman, 65 (3 May 1963), 683.

"For a Fatherless Son. "   Critical Quarterly, 5 (Summer
     1963), 115.

"Berck-Plage. "   London Magazine, New Series 3 (June 1963),
     26-31.

[Three Poems.] Poetry, 102 (August 1963), 292-298.
        "Fever 103° "
        "Purdah"
        "Eavesdropper"

[Seven Poems.] The New Yorker, 39 (3 August 1963), 28-29.
        "Two Campers in Cloud Country"
        "The Elm Speaks"
        "Mystic"
        "Amnesiac"
        "Mirror"
        "Among the Narcissi"
        "The Moon and the Yew Tree"

*"Ocean 1212-W. " The Listener, 70 (29 August 1963), 312-
        313.

"Ten Poems" (with a preface by Ted Hughes).   Encounter,
        21 (October 1963), 45-52.
        "Death & Co. "
        "The Swarm"
        "The Other"
        "Getting There"
        "Lady Lazarus"
        "Little Fugue"
        "Childless Woman"
        "The Jailor"
        "Thalidomide"
        "Daddy"

"The Last Poems of Sylvia Plath. " The Review, 9 (October
        1963), 4-19.
        "Daddy"
        "Lady Lazarus"
        "Fever 103° "
        "Ariel"
        "Poppies in October"
        "Nick and the Candlestick"
        "Brasilia"
        "Mary's Song"
        "Lesbos"

"Poppies in October. " The Observer, 6 October 1963, 24.

"The Horse. " The Observer, 3 November 1963, 22.

*The Bell Jar (under pseudonym of Victoria Lucas).   London:
        William Heinemann, 1963.

1964

[Two Poems.] New York Review of Books, 2 (20 February
    1964), 13.
        "The Munich Mannequins"
        "Totem"

*"The Wishing Box." Atlantic, 214 (October 1964), 86-89.

[Three Poems.] Critical Quarterly Supplement No. 5 (1964),
    2-4.
        "Daddy"
        "Small Hours"
        "In Plaster"

*"Ocean 1212-W." Writers on Themselves, introd. Herbert
    Read (London: BBC, 1964).

1965

"November Graveyard." Mademoiselle, 62 (November 1965),
    134.

[Two Poems.] Critical Quarterly Supplement No. 6 (1965),
    2-5.
        "The Bee Meeting"
        "Lady Lazarus"

Uncollected Poems. London: Turret Books, 1965. [Limited
    edition of 150 copies. With a jacket drawing by Syl-
    via Plath.]

Ariel. London: Faber & Faber, 1965.

1966

"An Appearance." Times Literary Supplement, 20 January
    1966, 42.

"Lesbos." New York Review of Books, 6 (12 May 1966),
    4-5.

"Daddy." Time, 87 (10 June 1966), 118.

"Selected Poems." Tri-Quarterly, 7 (Fall 1966), 11-38.
        "The Death of Mythmaking"

"Sow"
"Watercolor of Grantchester Meadows"
"The Colossus"
"Mushrooms"
"Sculptor"
"In Plaster"
"Lesbos"
"Words for a Nursery"
"Nick and the Candlestick"
"Stings"
"Fever 103° "
"Cut"
"The Bee Meeting"
"Death & Co. "
"Lady Lazarus"
"Daddy"
"Words"

*The Bell Jar. London: Faber & Faber, 1966. London:
       Faber & Faber, 1966 (paperback).

Ariel. New York: Harper & Row, 1966. New York: Har-
       per & Row, 1966 (paperback). [Both with a foreword
       by Robert Lowell.]

"Sylvia Plath. " In The Poet Speaks, ed. Peter Orr (London:
       Routledge & Kegan Paul; New York: Barnes & Noble),
       167-172. [Interview of 30 October 1962.]

1967

"Early Poems by Sylvia Plath. " Harvard Advocate, 101 (May
       1967), 2-3.
              "Danse Macabre"
              "Admonition"
              "Dialogue en Route"
              "Circus in Three Rings"
              "Mad Girl's Love Song"
              "Doomsday"

The Colossus. London: Faber & Faber, 1967.

1968

*"Eccentricity. " The Listener, 79 (9 May 1968), 607.

*"Johnny Panic and the Bible of Dreams." Atlantic, 222
(September 1968), 54-60.

"Two Poems." Critical Quarterly, 10 (Autumn 1968), 213-
214.
    Two passages from Three Women.

"Three Women: A Poem for Three Voices." Transatlantic
Review, 31 (Winter 1968-69), 51-52. [Excerpt.]

Three Women, A Monologue for Three Voices. London:
Turret Books, 1968. [Limited edition of 180 copies.
With a preface by Douglas Cleverdon.]

Ariel. London: Faber & Faber, 1968 (paperback).

The Colossus and Other Poems. New York: Random House,
1968 (paperback).

                          1969

"Early Poems by Sylvia Plath." Cambridge Review, 90 (7
February 1969), 244-245.
        "Street Song"
        "Natural History"
        "Resolve"
        "Aerialist"

"Early Unpublished Poems by Sylvia Plath." Times Literary
Supplement, 31 July 1969, 855.
        "Complaint of the Crazed Queen"
        "Battle-Scene from the Comic Operatic Fantasy
        'The Seafarer'"
        "Letter to a Purist"
        "Dream of the Hearse-Driver"
        "Dialogue en Route"

*"The Fifteen-Dollar Eagle." Penguin Modern Stories 2, ed.
Judith Burnley (Harmondsworth, England: Penguin,
1969).

"Three Women: A Poem for Three Voices." Quarterly Review of Literature, 16 (1969), 197-198. [Excerpt.]

*"Johnny Panic and the Bible of Dreams." Best American
Short Stories, ed. Foley and Burnett (Boston: Houghton Mifflin, 1969), 233-238.

1970

"Lyonnesse. "　The Observer, 10 May 1970, 31.

[Two Poems.]　Critical Quarterly, 12 (Summer 1970), 149-
150.
　　　"Two Campers in Cloud Country"
　　　"On Deck"

"Gigolo. "　The New Yorker, 46 (21 November 1970), 54.

[Selected Poems.]　In The Art of Sylvia Plath, ed. Charles
Newman (London:　Faber & Faber, 1970; Bloomington:
Indiana University Press, 1970).
　　　"On the Plethora of Dryads"
　　　"Words for a Nursery"
　　　"Mushrooms"
　　　"Purdah"
　　　"Mystic"
　　　"Three Women:　A Poem for Three Voices"
　　　　(Excerpts)
　　　"Thalidomide"
　　　"An Appearance"
　　　"Battle-Scene from the Comic Operatic Fantasy
　　　　'The Seafarer'"
　　　"Dialogue en Route"
　　　"Epitaph for Fire and Flower"
　　　"Half Moon"
　　　"In Plaster"
　　　"Lesbos"
　　　"Miss Drake Proceeds to Supper"

*"Ocean 1212-W. "　In The Art of Sylvia Plath, ed. Charles
Newman (London:　Faber & Faber; 1970; Bloomington:
Indiana University Press, 1970).

Wreath for a Bridal.　Frensham, England:　Sceptre Press,
1970. [Limited edition of 100 copies.]

1971

[Six Poems.]　The New Yorker, 47 (6 March 1971), 36-37.
　　　"Pheasant"
　　　"Babysitters"
　　　"The Courage of Shutting Up"
　　　"By Candlelight"

"For a Fatherless Son"
"Apprehensions"

"Stillborn. "   The New Statesman, 81 (19 March 1971), 384.

*"What I Found Out About Buddy Willard. "   McCall's, 98
  (April 1971), 86-87. [Excerpt from The Bell Jar.]

"The Tour. "   Times Literary Supplement, 28 May 1971, 610.

[Four Poems.]   London Magazine, New Series 11 (September
  1971), 41-46.
      "The Courage of Shutting Up"
      "For a Fatherless Son"
      "By Candlelight"
      "Gigolo"

[Three Poems.]   Mademoiselle, 73 (September 1971), 160-
  161.
      "The Surgeon at 2 a. m. "
      "Black Rook in Rainy Weather"
      "Stillborn"

[Three Poems.]   Intellectual Digest, 2 (November 1971), 95.
      "Edge"
      "Crossing the Water"
      "Lady Lazarus"

*"The Fifty-Ninth Bear. "   In Works in Progress, ed. Martha
  Saxton (New York: Literary Guild, 1971), 17-31.

*"Johnny Panic and the Bible of Dreams. "   In The Naked i,
  ed. Frederick R. Karl and Leo Hamalian (New York:
  Fawcett Books, 1971), 295-310.

Million Dollar Month.   Frensham, England: Sceptre Press,
  1971. [Limited edition of 150 copies.]

Child.   Exeter, England: Rougement Press, 1971. [Limited
  edition of 325 copies.]

Winter Trees.   London: Faber & Faber, 1971.

Crossing the Water.   London: Faber & Faber, 1971. New
  York: Harper & Row, 1971.

Lyonnesse.   London: Rainbow Press, 1971. [Limited edition
  of 400 copies.]

Crystal Gazer. London: Rainbow Press, 1971. [Limited
          edition of 400 copies. With a frontispiece drawing
          by Sylvia Plath.]

Fiesta Melons. Exeter, England: Rougement Press, 1971.
          [Limited edition of 150 copies. With an introduction
          by Ted Hughes and eleven drawings by Sylvia Plath.]

*The Bell Jar. New York: Harper & Row, 1971. [With a
          biographical note by Lois Ames and drawings by Sylvia
          Plath.]

1972

[Two Poems.] Mademoiselle, 74 (March 1972), 30.
          "Stopped Dead"
          "Winter Trees"

"Three Women: A Poem for Three Voices." Ms., 1 (Spring
          1972), 85-88. [Excerpt.]

"Metamorphosis." Poetry, 121 (October 1972), 25.

*"The Mother's Union." McCall's, 100 (October 1972), 80-
          81, 126, 128, 130, 142.

Winter Trees. New York: Harper & Row, 1972.

*The Bell Jar. New York: Bantam, 1972 (paperback).
          [With a biographical note by Lois Ames and drawings
          by Sylvia Plath.]

The Colossus. London: Faber & Faber, 1972 (paperback).

1973

"Morning Song." Redbook, 140 (January 1973), 76.

*"The Day Mr. Prescott Died." Spare Rib, June 1973.

Pursuit. London: Rainbow Press, 1973. [Limited edition
          of 100 copies. With an introduction by Ted Hughes
          and etchings by Leonard Baskin.]

1974

"Ode to a Bitten Plum. " Seventeen, 33 (January 1974), 136.

"Three Women: A Poem for Three Voices. " Quarterly Re-
    view of Literature, 19 (1974), 447-448. [Excerpt.]

1975

*"Sylvia Plath on Her Love and Marriage. " Mademoiselle,
    81 (July 1975), 82-87. [Excerpts from Letters Home.]

*Letters Home: Correspondence 1950-1963, edited and with
    commentary by Aurelia Schober Plath. New York:
    Harper and Row, 1975.

Crossing the Water. New York: Harper & Row, 1975 (pa-
    perback); London: Faber & Faber, 1975 (paperback).

Winter Trees. London: Faber & Faber, 1975 (paperback).

1976

The Bed Book. London; Faber & Faber, 1976. Text by
    Sylvia Plath; Illustrations by Quentin Blake. New
    York: Harper and Row, 1970. Text by Sylvia Plath;
    Pictures by Emily Arnold McCully.

1977

*Letters Home: Correspondence 1950-1963, edited and with
    commentary by Aurelia Schober Plath. New York:
    Bantam Books, 1977 (paperback).

*Johnny Panic and the Bible of Dreams. London: Faber &
    Faber, 1977. [With an introduction by Ted Hughes.]

B. DIFFERENCES IN THE AMERICAN AND BRITISH EDITIONS OF THE FOUR MAJOR BOOKS OF PLATH'S POEMS

THE COLOSSUS

British: London: William Heinemann, 1960.
             London: Faber & Faber, 1967.
             London: Faber & Faber, 1972 (paperback).

American: New York: Alfred A. Knopf, 1962.
           New York: Random House, 1968 (paperback).

The American editions lack ten poems printed in the British:
     Metaphors
     Black Rook in Rainy Weather
     Maudlin
     Ouija
     Two Sisters of Persephone
     Who
     Dark House
     Maenad
     The Beast
     Witch Burning

ARIEL

British: London: Faber & Faber, 1965.
             London: Faber & Faber, 1968 (paperback).

American: New York: Harper & Row, 1966.
           New York: Harper & Row, 1966 (paperback).

The British editions lack three poems printed in the American:
     Lesbos
     Mary's Song
     The Swarm

CROSSING THE WATER

British: London: Faber & Faber, 1971.
             London: Faber & Faber, 1975 (paperback).

American: New York: Harper & Row, 1971.
             New York: Harper & Row, 1975 (paperback).

The British editions lack ten poems printed in the American:
        Black Rook in Rainy Weather
        Metaphors
        Maudlin
        Ouija
        Two Sisters of Persephone
        Who
        Dark House
        Maenad
        The Beast
        Witch Burning

The American editions lack six poems printed in the British:
        Pheasant
        An Appearance
        Event
        Apprehensions
        Tho Tour
        Among the Narcissi

WINTER TREES

British: London: Faber & Faber, 1971.
             London: Faber & Faber, 1975 (paperback).

American: New York: Harper & Row, 1972.

The British editions lack nine poems printed in the American:
        Apprehensions
        An Appearance
        The Detective
        Among the Narcissi
        Event
        Amnesiac
        Eavesdropper
        Pheasant
        The Tour

The American edition lacks three poems printed in the
      British:
            Lesbos
            The Swarm
            Mary's Song

Summary

Except for three poems, the overall contents of the British
and American Books of Plath's poems are identical. Those
three, never printed in Britain, are:
            The Detective
            Amnesiac
            Eavesdropper

C. WORKS FORTHCOMING

Primary

A collected edition of Sylvia Plath's poems is due to appear in 1978 or 1979. It will be published in England by Faber & Faber and in America by Harper and Row.

An American edition of Plath's selected prose, Johnny Panic and the Bible of Dreams, and Other Prose Works, is due from Harper & Row in 1978.

Secondary

Although several critical studies are known to be in progress, we know of none in press. A major chapter on Plath will appear in the late Arthur Oberg's forthcoming book on the lyric (Rutgers University Press).

A collection of new critical essays, edited by Gary Lane, will appear in 1978 from the Johns Hopkins University Press.

Two critical biographies are in progress, Lois Ames' authorized biography and another by Harriet Rosenstein. Both have been under contract and in progress for some time, but no publication dates are presently set.

D. SELECTED ANTHOLOGIES IN WHICH PLATH'S POEMS APPEAR

A Book of Comfort: An Anthology. Ed. Elizabeth Goudge.
New York: Coward-McCann, 1974.
Kindness

A Book of Nature Poems. Ed. William Cole. New York:
Viking, 1969.
Mushrooms

The College Anthology of British and American Poetry. 2nd
edition. Ed. A. Kent Hieatt and William Park. Boston: Allyn, 1972.
Ariel
Cut

A College Book of Verse. Ed. C. F. Main. Belmont, California: Wadsworth, 1970.
The Hanging Man
Morning Song

Contemporary American Poetry. 2nd edition. Ed. A. Poulin,
Jr. Boston: Houghton Mifflin, 1975.
Brasilia
The Colossus
Cut
Daddy
Lady Lazarus
Mary's Song
Medusa
Nick and the Candlestick
The Stones
Winter Trees

The Contemporary American Poets: American Poetry Since
1940. Ed. Mark Strand. New York, World Publishing, 1969.

Daddy
The Moon and the Yew Tree
Nick and the Candlestick

The Experience of Poems: A Text and Anthology. Ed. and
    prepared by John O. Perry. New York: Macmillan,
    1972.
    Ariel

50 Modern American and British Poets: 1920-1970. Ed.
    Louis Untermeyer. New York: David McKay, 1973.
    The Applicant
    Daddy
    Morning Song

A Flock of Words. Ed. David Mackay. New York: Har-
    court, Brace and World, 1969.
    Child

The Golden Year: The Poetry Society of America Anthology,
    1910-1960. Ed. Melville Cane, John Farrar, and
    Louise Townsend Nicholl. New York: Fine Editions
    Press, 1960.
    Hardcastle Crags
    Two Views of a Cadaver Room

The Honey and the Gall: Poems of Married Life. Ed. Chad
    Walsh. New York: Macmillan, 1967.
    The Applicant

A Little Treasury of Modern Poetry, English and American.
    3rd edition. Ed. Oscar Williams. New York: Scrib-
    ner's, 1970.
    Black Rook in Rainy Weather
    The Colossus
    Daddy

Male and Female: Identity. Ed. John Harrington. New
    York: Wiley, 1972.
    The Jailor

Modern Poems: An Introduction to Poetry. Ed. Richard
    Ellmann and Robert O'Clair. New York: Norton,
    1976.
    Ariel
    Daddy
    Lady Lazarus

The Modern Poets. 2nd edition. Ed. John Malcolm Brinnin
  and Bill Read, with photos by Rollie McKenna. New
  York: McGraw-Hill, 1970.
    The Applicant
    Daddy

Naked Poetry: Recent American Poetry in Open Forms. Ed.
  Stephen Berg and Robert Mezey. Indianapolis: Bobbs-
  Merrill, 1969.
    The Applicant
    The Arrival of the Bee Box
    Daddy
    Lady Lazarus
    The Moon and the Yew Tree
    The Munich Mannequins
    Poppies in July
    Sheep in Fog
    Stings
    Tulips

The New Poetry. Ed. M. L. Rosenthal. New York: Mac-
  millan, 1967.
    Ariel
    Daddy
    Fever 103°
    Suicide off Egg Rock
    Two Views of a Cadaver Room

New Poets of England and America. 2nd selection. Ed. Donald Hall and Robert Pack. New York: World Publishing, 1962.
    Black Rook in Rainy Weather
    Blue Moles
    The Colossus
    The Ghost's Leavetaking
    Mushrooms
    Snakecharmer

The New Yorker Book of Poems. Selected by the editors of
  The New Yorker. New York: William Morrow, 1974.
    Amnesiac
    Blackberrying
    The Elm Speaks
    Mirror
    The Moon and the Yew Tree
    Mussel Hunter at Rock Harbor
    Mystic

Night Walk
Tulips
Two Campers in Cloud Country
Water Color of Grantchester Meadows

The Norton Anthology of Modern Poetry. Ed. Richard Ell-
    mann and Robert O'Clair. New York: Norton, 1973.
    Ariel
    Blackberrying
    The Colossus
    Daddy
    Elm
    Fever 103°
    Lady Lazarus
    Poppies in October

The Norton Anthology of Poetry. Revised edition. Ed. Ar-
    thur M. Eastman et al. New York: Norton, 1975.
    Ariel
    Black Rook in Rainy Weather
    Lady Lazarus
    Tulips

The Norton Anthology of Poetry. Ed. Arthur M. Eastman et
    al. New York: Norton, 1970.
    Medallion
    Point Shirley
    The Rival

100 Postwar Poems. Ed. M. L. Rosenthal. New York:
    Macmillan, 1968.
    Ariel
    Daddy
    Death & Co.

The Poem: An Anthology. Ed. Stanley B. Greenfield and
    A. Kingsley Weatherhead. New York: Appleton-Cen-
    tury-Crofts, 1968.
    Blue Moles
    The Elm

Poems of Doubt and Belief: An Anthology of Modern Religious
    Poetry. Ed. Tom F. Driver and Robert Pack. New
    York: Macmillan, 1964.
    Black Rook in Rainy Weather

Poems of Our Moment: Contemporary Poets of the English

Language.   Ed. John Hollander.   Indianapolis: Pega-
sus, 1968.
    The Arrival of the Bee Box
    The Bee Meeting
    Death & Co.
    The Night Dances

Poems on Poetry: The Mirror's Garland.   Ed. Robert Wal-
    lace and James G. Taaffe.   New York: Dutton, 1965.
    Black Rook in Rainy Weather
    Snakecharmer

Poetry: An Introductory Anthology.   Ed. Hazard Adams.
    Boston: Little, Brown, 1968.
    Tulips

Possibilities of Poetry: An Anthology of American Contem-
    poraries.   New York: Dale, 1970.
    The Applicant
    The Colossus
    Daddy
    Elm
    Lady Lazarus
    Suicide off Egg Rock
    Tulips

Psyche: The Feminine Poetic Consciousness: An Anthology
    of Modern American Women Poets.   Ed. Barbara
    Segnitz and Carol Rainey.   New York: Dial Press,
    1973.
    The Applicant
    Ariel
    Black Rook in Rainy Weather
    The Colossus
    Daddy
    Kindness
    Lady Lazarus
    Mushrooms
    Tulips

To Play Man Number One.   Ed. Sara Hannum and John Ter-
    ry Chase.   New York: Atheneum, 1969.
    The Arrival of the Bee Box
    Balloons

AUTHOR INDEX

PERIODICAL INDEX